Ian Bradley is Emeritus Professor of Cultural and Spiritual History at the University of St Andrews. He is a Trustee of the Scottish Pilgrim Routes Forum and has been closely involved with the Fife Pilgrim Way since its conception. Among his many other books are *Pilgrimage: A Cultural and Spiritual Journey* (2009), *Argyll: The Making of a Spiritual Landscape* (St Andrew Press, 2015) and *Following the Celtic Way* (Darton, Longman & Todd, 2018).

# THE
# FIFE
# PILGRIM
# WAY

## IN THE FOOTSTEPS OF MONKS, MINERS AND MARTYRS

### IAN BRADLEY

First published in 2019 by
Birlinn Limited
West Newington House
10 Newington Road
Edinburgh
EH9 1QS

www.birlinn.co.uk

2

ISBN 978 178027 592 5

British Library Cataloguing
in Publication Data
A catalogue record for this book
is available from the British Library.

Designed and typeset by
Mark Blackadder

Printed and bound by PNB, Latvia

# Contents

PART 3
Reaching the destination: St Andrews,
the haunted city of relics and reformers

# Acknowledgements

I have benefited considerably from the friendship and encouragement of fellow founder members and trustees of the Scottish Pilgrim Routes Forum, especially the indefatigable and inspirational Nick Cooke, John Henderson, Roger Pickering, David Atkinson and Sheila Kesting. Fellow members of the ACTS Fife Pilgrim Way Steering Group have also been very supportive, notably Douglas Galbraith and Alan Kimmett. Ed Heather-Hayes and Miranda Lorraine from Fife Coast and Countryside Trust have been consistently helpful and encouraging. Tom Turpie generously allowed me to use and quote from the background notes which he produced for the Fife Pilgrim Way, Sheila Pitcairn shared with me her interesting and important work on Dunfermline as a place of pilgrimage and Giles Dove has let me quote from his fascinating St Andrews MPhil dissertation on 'Saints, Dedications and Cults in Medieval Fife'.

In St Andrews, Bess Rhodes has been very helpful in sharing her knowledge of the Reformation and her infectious enthusiasm for the history of the cathedral. It was a joy to supervise Dawn Laing on a dissertation on the Fife Pilgrim Way. Clergy, worship leaders and church guardians along the route have opened their churches to me and helped me with queries, notably Jim Campbell at Ceres Parish Church, Alasdair Coles at All Saints' Episcopal Church, St Andrews, Alan Kimmett at St Columba's Church, Glenrothes, Colin Alston at St Peter's Church, Inverkeithing, Fr Chris Heenan at St Margaret

Memorial Church, Dunfermline, Fraser Munro at the Arnot Gospel Hall, Kennoway, Gordon Mitchell, Session Clerk of Kinglassie Parish Church, Leslie Barr in Kelty, Ian Brown and George Seath from Ballingry and Rosemary Wallace and Robert Martin from Auchterderran.

I learned much on a wonderful walk from Glenrothes to Markinch led by Bruce Manson, who has also helped me with historical queries about Markinch. A talk in St Andrews on pilgrim badges by Gavin Grant, Collections Team Leader with Fife Cultural Trust, and a lecture on the architecture of St Andrews Cathedral by Julian Luxford of the History of Art School at St Andrews University were also very helpful. David Thomson arranged a very useful meeting with members of Kinglassie Pilgrim Way and Heritage Group and Sandy Russell kindly let me borrow his rich collection of material on West Fife's mining heritage. Catherine Stihler first alerted me to the importance, and the neglect, of the Battle of Inverkeithing. Paula Martin shared her knowledge of the history of Ceres with me, while Dave Reid put me right about where Archbishop Sharp may have spent his last night in Kennoway and Bill Hyland enlightened me about the life of the Augustinian canons. George Corbett, with whom I shared a walk on the Kennoway to Ceres stretch of the Pilgrim Way, shared his interesting theory about the origin of the name Ceres and offered other interesting information on the area.

Andrew Simmons and the whole team at Birlinn have been very supportive and helpful. I am grateful to Michael Brown and Katie Stevenson for permission to reproduce the extract from *Medieval St Andrews* (Boydell Press, 2017) quoted in chapter 10, and to Rosemary Wallace and Robert Martin for allowing me to quote the paragraph from *Auchterderran Kirk* (2016) reproduced in chapter 7.

Generous subventions from the Fife Coast and Countryside Trust and the Strathmartine Trust have contributed towards the provision of colour illustrations throughout this book, and their financial support is gratefully acknowledged. The map reproduced on pp. 10–11 was drawn by Jenny Proudfoot.

All photographic illustrations in this book are by the author except for those listed below, which are reproduced by kind permission of the copyright holders: pp. 2–3 John Murray; p. 12 Fife Coast and Countryside Trust; p.29 lower: Fife Cultural Trust; pp. 30–1 DGB/Alamy Stock Photo; p. 35 Kraft-stoff/Shutterstock; pp. 56–7 Carnegie Dunfermline Trust; p. 79 Historic Environment Scotland; p. 168 upper: John Murray; pp. 194–5 Mary McLeron/Alamy Stock Photo; p. 225 University of St Andrews; p. 251 upper: alanf/Shutterstock; p. 251 lower: MSP Travel Images/Alamy Stock Photo; p. 253 upper: John Stewart; p. 257 S.K. Reid Photography; pp. 266–7 Sarah Kennedy, Smart History, University of St Andrews; p. 270 Mike Wragg.

FIFE

KINGLASSIE

LOCHORE

GER

MARKINCH

DUNFERMLINE

INVERKEITHING

CULROSS

NORTH QUEENSFERRY

St Serf's Island

Scotlandwell

Kinglassie

Glenrothe

Lochore Meadows

Dunfermline

Inverkeithing

Culross

North Queensferry

Kennoway

Clatto

Ceres

Craigtoun

St Andrews

Earlsferry

FIRTH OF FORTH

# Introduction

Fife was long known as the pilgrim kingdom. This is because within its bounds were found the two most important places of pilgrimage in medieval Scotland, Dunfermline (which was also the residence of successive Scottish monarchs – hence the kingdom designation) and St Andrews. At the height of the pilgrimage boom in the Middle Ages, thousands of people from many parts of the British Isles and beyond traversed Fife to venerate the shrines of St Margaret and St Andrew. In the words of the medieval historian Tom Turpie, 'The economy, communication networks, landscape and religious and cultural life of Fife, perhaps more than any other region of medieval Scotland, was shaped by the presence of pilgrims and the veneration of saints' (Turpie 2016: 4).

Opposite
Path to
Kinglassie Well

The Fife Pilgrim Way, officially opened in July 2019, allows modern pilgrims to follow in the wake of their medieval predecessors and walk, cycle or otherwise make their way across Fife towards St Andrews on a route that has two starting points on the northern shores of the Firth of Forth: Culross, with its associations with two early Scottish saints, and North Queensferry, where Queen Margaret established the ferry crossing for pilgrims going to St Andrews. It is based on the premise that following in the footsteps of medieval pilgrims across Fife is a great way to discover the region's remarkable past, its lively modern communities, countryside, historic towns and natural treasures. But it is much more than an exercise in historical reconstruction. For a start, it does not follow the route taken by most medieval pilgrims who would have gone directly north from Kelty to Loch Leven and travelled on via Scotlandwell, taking a more northerly course. The modern pilgrim way has been deliberately routed through old mining and industrial areas of West Fife and the new town of Glenrothes. This is partly in the hope of bringing economic and other benefits to places which have experienced decline and do not see many visitors or tourists, as has happened in Galicia in Spain, the site of Europe's most famous pilgrim way, the Camino de Santiago, which leads to the shrine of St James.

There is also a conscious desire that those journeying along the Fife Pilgrim Way will not only see pretty vistas and affluent villages, but also come into contact with places and people that have not been so favoured. In a phrase generally attributed, probably wrongly, to King James VI and I, Fife has been described as 'a beggar's mantle fringed with gold'. The golden coastal fringe, with its quaint fishing villages and breathtaking views across the Forth, has long been the route of a hugely popular walk developed and maintained by Fife Coast and Countryside Trust. The Fife Pilgrim Way allows people to explore and encounter the beggar's mantle, not so immediately and obviously appealing as the coast, but packed with historical, social and spiritual interest. It has been developed through a partnership between churches of all denominations, local history and heritage groups and others interested in the practice of pilgrimage brought together by the Scottish Pilgrim Routes Forum, which had its very first meeting in the old manse in Culross in 2012. Fife Council has been strongly supportive of the project from the beginning, and Fife Coast and Countryside Trust, an independent environmental charity spun off from the Council's Rangers service, has been responsible for route-planning, way-marking, interpretation and marketing. It is appropriate that the first meeting of the Fife Pilgrim Way Network, bringing together interested parties from the churches, the local authority, voluntary organisations and others, took place on 11 July 2012 in Committee Room 1 of Fife Council's headquarters at Fife House in Glenrothes.

The logo chosen for the Fife Pilgrim Way, which appears on the front cover of this book and on all signposts, maps, guides and promotional material, is based on a fifteenth-century lead alloy pilgrim badge discovered during excavations at St Andrews Castle in 1998 (see p. 29). It depicts the apostle Andrew, one of the first disciples called by Christ, being crucified on the diagonal cross on which he is said to have been bound rather than nailed in order to prolong his suffering. For the logo, a crown has been added at the top, to represent Fife's royal connections and specifically the royal palace at Dunfermline, where many prominent Scottish kings and queens were born and laid to rest. Beneath the figure of the saint another image has been added in the form of the distinctive cross found carved into the inner wall of the tower in Markinch Parish Church, which stands roughly at the halfway point of the 64-mile long route and is one of the most interesting church buildings along it. The two round holes on the left-hand side of the badge are where it would have been sewn onto the hat or cloak of a pilgrim. On the other side, the frame or border is missing, as it is in the original badge, which is now on display alongside other pilgrim badges in the Kinburn House Museum in St Andrews. This gap conveniently allows the words 'Fife Pilgrim Way' to be inserted and form part of the design. It also points to the brokenness of pilgrims, many of whom set out on their travels to seek forgiveness for sins and come to terms with failings. All pilgrims are in some sense 'the walking wounded', carrying their hurts, guilt, unresolved tensions, unease and fears. The missing border of the pilgrim badge also points to the incompleteness of every earthly journey. We set out only to come back again, and every departure involves a return until we make the pilgrimage that awaits each and every one of us as we depart from this world.

The practice of pilgrimage, understood as a departure from daily life on a journey with a spiritual intention, and often – although not invariably – to a destination with a religious significance, is a central feature of all the world's major faiths. It is not obligatory for Christians but it has long been a significant aspect of Christian life and devotion.

Jesus sent out his disciples to preach the kingdom of God and to heal, telling them to go from house to house, taking nothing on their journey. Some early Christians, like the Celtic monks who wandered across continental Europe as well as around the remoter shores of the British Isles, took to almost perpetual pilgrimage as a demanding form of witness and exiled themselves from home comforts as they sought to follow the Son of Man who had nowhere to lay his head. The desire to walk in Jesus' footsteps led other early Christians to journey to the Holy Land. As the cult of saints developed and certain places came to be seen as especially sacred, Christian pilgrimage reached its zenith in the Middle Ages, with thousands travelling for many months across Europe to Rome, Santiago, St Andrews, Dunfermline and other shrines associated with apostles, saints and martyrs.

Pilgrimage effectively ceased in Scotland with the Reformation. In fact, there is considerable evidence that St Andrews was in significant decline as a pilgrim destination fifty years or so before Protestantism was officially established in 1560. For the next 400 years and more pilgrimage and pilgrim places largely disappeared across Scotland as they did across the whole of Protestant Europe. The Reformers had good and understandable reasons for attacking the practice of pilgrimage, which had become associated with the buying and selling of indulgences and the idea of paying your way into heaven. The result was that pilgrimage became almost a dirty word in Scotland, at least in Presbyterian circles.

In the last three or four decades something remarkable has happened. There has been a widespread and striking revival of interest in the practice of pilgrimage across Europe. Somewhat surprisingly, perhaps, given its reputation for Presbyterian disapproval of the more Catholic practices of the Middle Ages, Scotland is in the van of this movement, with more new pilgrim routes being created here than in any other part of the United Kingdom. Significant initiatives across the country have been stimulated by a combination of local enthusiasm and support from the Scottish Government and local authorities keen to promote health, well-being and economic regeneration, as well as revived interest in local saints, and the Scottish Pilgrim Routes Forum's efforts to bring together interested parties within churches, heritage groups and the tourism sector. Lingering Presbyterian unease has at last been put to rest, not least by a spectacular vote of confidence at the 2017 General Assembly of the Church of Scotland, which passed with acclamation a deliverance from its Church and Society Council affirming the place of pilgrimage within the life of the Church and encouraging congregations to explore opportunities for pilgrimage locally and the provision of practical and spiritual support for pilgrims passing through their parishes.

The Fife Pilgrim Way is one of six major walking and cycling pilgrimage routes currently being developed across Scotland by steering groups made up of local enthusiasts, churches, voluntary bodies and local authorities. Many of these volunteers represent member organisations of the Scottish Pilgrim Routes Forum, a national network set up in 2012 and a fully constituted Scottish charity which supports and facilitates the work of the steering groups and meets twice a year in locations closely associated with their work. The most ambitious of the new pilgrim ways will be a 185-mile coast-to-coast route linking Iona and St Andrews, two of Scotland's most iconic religious sites and places of medieval pilgrimage. The second longest, initially created in 2013 by a group of enthusiasts from Paisley Abbey, is the 149-mile Whithorn Way from Glasgow to Whithorn, once the site of a major cathedral associated with St Ninian and an important place of pilgrimage since the seventh century. The 72-mile Forth to Farne Way, linking North Berwick to Lindisfarne, opened in 2017. In north-east Scotland, the 40-mile Deeside Way follows the route of the old railway track between Aberdeen and Ballater. The most northerly of the new pilgrimage routes is the St Magnus Way, a 55-mile walking trail across mainland Orkney from Evie to Kirkwall, opened in 2017 to mark the 900th anniversary of the martyrdom of Orkney's patron saint. The development of these six routes represents the beginning of a long-term strategy co-ordinated by the Scottish Pilgrim Routes Forum to create opportunities for local people and overseas visitors alike to learn from and experience Scotland's rich pilgrimage heritage through the outdoor environment.

Those who use the Fife Pilgrim Way, whether to make the whole 64-mile trek on foot or to travel along a short section by bicycle, wheelchair or other means of transport, will have many different motivations. For some it will be primarily to take some exercise, get some fresh air, enjoy the countryside or explore historic sites. Others may have, or come to have, more spiritual reasons for undertaking pilgrimage. Before beginning to explore the route in terms of its historical and spiritual significance, it is worth briefly examining the motives that have taken people on pilgrimage in the past and what the differences are between medieval and modern pilgrims.

If we are going to begin to enter into the medieval pilgrim's mindset we need to appreciate the overwhelming fear of death, judgement, Hell and damnation that was universal throughout Europe in the Middle Ages. We can gain some sense of this from those terrifying images of the Last Judgement and the eternal torments of Hell found on so many wall paintings in medieval churches. Medieval Christians lived in perpetual fear of being condemned as a sinner at the Last Judgement and being cast into the fiery furnaces of everlasting damnation. The (almost literally) burning question for them was 'What must I do to be saved?' This was what inspired their attitude of penitence, understood as contrition, repentance and resolve to atone for their misdemeanours and obtain God's forgiveness. It also underlay the complex system of penances established by the Church. These were prescribed penalties for sins which, taken together with earnest and sincere repentance and resolve to live better lives, were believed to mitigate the chances of facing damnation and secure the real possibility of salvation and entrance into heaven.

It is against this background of a prevailing attitude of penitence and the performance of numerous penances imposed by the Church that we need to understand medieval pilgrimage. Many pilgrims saw themselves first and foremost as penitents – they left home, often on long, uncomfortable, unpredictable and perilous journeys, in a spirit of penitence and in an effort to cleanse their souls and atone for their sins and failings – in some ways the more uncomfortable and hazardous the pilgrim journey, the better it was and the more likely to benefit those undertaking it in terms of a cleansing and purgative experience. Many pilgrims were also actually serving out penances prescribed by the Church or by the civil authorities. Medieval Scottish courts had the power to require those convicted of homicide to make a pilgrimage on foot to one of the shrines of the head saints of Scotland, of whom Andrew was the most prominent. The churches also regularly imposed a pilgrimage as a penance on someone who had confessed a sin to a priest or bishop. Several pilgrims came to St Andrews from continental Europe having been prescribed the journey there as a penance by local civil or ecclesiastical courts (see p. 213).

It was this penitential aspect of pilgrimage, and this overriding fear of death, judgement, Hell and damnation, that led to the development of the whole apparatus of indulgences which became so associated with late medieval pilgrimage and which so damned it in the eyes of the Protestant Reformers. The doctrine of Purgatory developed in the early Middle Ages to provide some kind of hope for those, the great majority of the population probably, who felt that they could never properly atone in this life for the sins that they had committed and feared that however penitential they were and however many penances they performed, they would still be found guilty at the terrible judgement seat and committed to perdition. Purgatory provided a second chance, a kind of halfway house between this world and the next, a post-mortem state of existence which allowed souls to be purified and refined and cleaned before facing the last judgement. It was envisaged in temporal terms and often seen as being a long haul. Indulgences, which came to be sold by the Church to raise money for building and other projects, allowed people to shorten their time in Purgatory, speed up the process of spring-cleaning their souls and get to the Day of Judgement more quickly and also in a more spick and span state. Undertaking a prescribed pilgrimage was one of the main ways of gaining an indulgence.

That is one reason why people went on pilgrimage. Another takes us to a second striking feature of the medieval mindset which is difficult for us to grasp today – its fascination and obsession with saints and relics. The cult of saints arose as the years and the centuries passed from the time of Jesus and the apostles, and a need seems to have been felt for more recent holy men and women as role models and objects of reverence and honour. Martyrdom played a key part in the creation of saints – those who had died for their faith became especially venerated. In many areas, not least Scotland, local saints were important. Along with the cult of saints came the cult of relics and corporeal remains. This stemmed from a very physical and literal approach to the faith, where people believed that by touching, or even seeing or being in close proximity to the bones, clothes or other objects associated with the saints, they would somehow pick up some of the spiritual power and aura of these superhuman and super-holy men and women. This idea was expressed in the widespread belief that in death the saints performed posthumous miracles, especially miracles of healing. The performance of miracles was, and still remains in the Roman Catholic Church today, a key determinant of sanctity – and it was the miracles that were widely reported as taking place at and around saints' shrines which drew many people to them.

Saints' shrines, especially, drew those seeking healing and relief from pain and suffering, whether physical, mental or spiritual, both for themselves and for others. Many medieval pilgrims fell into this category. People also made pilgrimages in the Middle Ages to give thanks for deliverance from pain, for the birth of children or for good harvests and other blessings and benefits. Quite often these pilgrimages of thanks were made in fulfilment of vows that the pilgrims had made earlier when they had prayed for deliverance.

So there were a number of spiritual motives which took people on pilgrimage in the Middle Ages – penitence, penance, accessing the power of the saints still latent in their physical remains and relics, seeking physical and psychological healing, giving thanks and generally benefiting the soul and bringing one closer to Heaven. But it is clear also that many pilgrims were motivated by rather less exalted and less spiritual impulses. They were more like modern tourists and holiday-makers. Pilgrimage provided just about the only opportunity available for most people in the Middle Ages to leave the confines of their home village, their family and the ties that bound them. It meant adventure, new sights, meeting new people and getting away from the abusive husband, the nagging wife or the meddling parish priest.

The motives that take people on pilgrimages today are as many and various as they were in the Middle Ages, and perhaps not quite as different as we might think. The quest for a deeper spirituality and for mental, physical and psychological healing is mixed with a sense of adventure, a desire to get out of the rut, broaden horizons and enjoy a new and different experience. Pilgrimages are still undertaken with a penitential purpose, as part of an attempt to reorientate lives away from selfishness and make a new start, to face challenges and experience, if only temporarily, a simpler and less comfortable lifestyle. Of course, there is nothing like the same fear of Hell and judgement today as there was in the Middle Ages. The decline of belief in Hell was one of the most significant theological trends in the nineteenth century, and it has continued apace since then. But that does not mean that people are not dissatisfied or uneasy about their lives and lifestyles – indeed, in some ways we are perhaps even less at ease with ourselves and more prone to angst and self-doubt than our medieval ancestors were. For not a few pilgrims today, especially those undertaking a long and rigorous walk like the Camino de Santiago, part of the motivation is a cleansing of the soul, although some might not put it in quite those terms, and a desire for a period and process of self-examination and reorientation, often coupled with a yearning for a simpler and less selfish lifestyle.

There is a strong sense of shared community about taking part in a pilgrimage which many people welcome in our increasingly atomised and individualistic culture. Pilgrims form egalitarian and inclusive communities in which individuals are temporarily freed of the hierar-chical roles and status which they bear in everyday life. I vividly recall the first words of our leader when my wife and I joined a group of pilgrims walking the St Olav Way to Trondheim. As we were about to introduce ourselves, he said: 'It is not important where we come from or what jobs we do. For the next week we are all simply pilgrims.'

Pilgrimage is often undertaken today to mark a significant birthday or anniversary, or an important landmark in life such as retirement. Part of the reason why the number of people making a pilgrimage is on the increase is undoubtedly because of the growing appeal of sabbaticals, gap years and taking time out from ever more stressed lives. There are also still those who are primarily motivated by a desire to give thanks or seek healing. The current revival of interest in the practice of pilgrimage ties in with the recovery of a sense of the sacredness of place and landscape in an increasingly fragile and urbanised world, and the growing emphasis on physical well-being and exercise. This is a further significant motive for many of today's pilgrims, and it is why bodies like the Scottish Government and local authorities support the development of pilgrim ways as an aspect of their strategies to combat obesity, promote physical fitness and encourage exercise. Pilgrimage also ties in with the widespread desire today to rediscover and connect with roots, traditions and history, especially local history – which is why some of the most enthusiastic partners in the creation of Scottish pilgrim routes have been local history, heritage and conservation groups.

Many people find it easier to walk rather than talk their faith, and find encouragement through treading in the footsteps of countless pilgrims before them. Walking has clear psychological as well as physical benefits, as St Jerome discerned in the fourth century in his observation *solvitur ambulando* (it can be solved by walking). An experienced Christian therapist has shared with me how beneficial it can be for people to make confession, formal or otherwise, and get things off their chest while walking side by side with a companion/confessor rather than in a more confrontational face-to-face encounter. I have certainly experienced some of the deepest and most profound conversations of my life while walking alongside a fellow pilgrim, often someone whom I did not know and did not expect to meet again.

There are also numerous pilgrims today, as there were in the Middle Ages, who are impelled by a sense of adventure, or wanderlust, and who are perhaps as much tourists as pilgrims. But we need to be careful about making too hard and fast a distinction between these two categories. The dividing line between pilgrims and tourists has long been blurred, and is becoming more so. It has been said that while tourists return from their travels with souvenirs, pilgrims come back with blessings. Yet pilgrims have long picked up souvenirs, like the badges depicting Andrew and other saints that were mass-produced between the twelfth and fifteenth centuries to be sewn on to hats and cloaks, and many modern camera-toting and coach-borne visitors to churches and sacred places pause to light a candle and pray. If some of what passes for pilgrimage today is really tourism, it is also the case that many modern tourists are searching for something beyond a holiday. This provides a great opportunity for the Church today to help tourists become pilgrims.

Pilgrimage has much to offer an age such as ours where there is so much anxiety, stress, yearning and seeking. It fits the needs of a restless generation – but perhaps restlessness is, in fact, part of the human condition. Bruce Chatwin, the travel writer, has suggested in his book *Songlines* that humans are born to be nomads and that our natural inclinations turn us towards movement and journeying. The desire to be pilgrims reflects yearnings to find a deeper purpose and meaning in our lives. It also chimes with the way that increasing numbers of people see their faith. Surveys suggest that far more Christians now describe their faith as an ongoing journey rather than as a sudden decisive conversion experience. The road to Emmaus, along which the resurrected Jesus travelled with two of his disciples for many miles before they recognised him, seems to resonate with more believers nowadays than the road to Damascus, where Paul underwent a sudden blinding conversion.

The Latin word *peregrinus*, from which the word pilgrim is derived, means a stranger or traveller (literally *per ager*, or through the land).

Pilgrimage is a provisional, transitory state, often taken as a metaphor for the journey of life, hastening irrevocably from the cradle to the grave. It is a reminder that all things in this world are temporary and that everything is in motion, nothing is ever static. In several religious traditions, pilgrimages to remote places are often undertaken towards the end of life to prepare for death by stripping away the comforts and distractions of this world. For some, pilgrimage is a perpetual state of life, as it was for the wandering Irish monks of the Dark Ages and is now for the Hindu *sadhus* who have renounced the world and perpetually travel from one shrine to another. For most of us, however, pilgrimage is an occasional rather than a perpetual state – one for which we prepare and from which we return in some small way changed, healed, refreshed and enriched, with our horizons broadened. In practical terms, it gives those of us who are not monks or free spirits, who are tied to the responsibilities and obligations that come with family or employment, the chance to leave our settled routines for a while, walk in the footsteps of the saints and the faithful of countless ages and find new companions on the way.

It has been said that one of the differences between tourists and pilgrims is that while the former pass through places, the latter allow places to pass through and affect them, with more engagement with those whom they meet on the way and in whose footsteps they are travelling. That is why this book has much about the customs, lives and beliefs of those people who have lived and worked and walked over the centuries along the route taken by the Fife Pilgrim Way today. Some pilgrim routes go through wild, spectacular remote scenery and have long stretches where there is little but raw nature and untamed wilderness. The Fife Pilgrim Way is not like that – you are never far from civilisation and the landscape is for the most part either urban, post-industrial or agricultural. Fife's only significant relatively remote and mountain wilderness-like area, the Lomond Hills, is not on the route. This means that there are ample opportunities along the way to interact with people and communities, their stories, their roots, their faith and doubts. The old saying, 'It taks a lang spoon tae sup wi' a Fifer', might be taken to suggest that the inhabitants of Fife are somewhat unfriendly and inhospitable. Behind the reserve and what can sometimes seem like dourness, there is, in fact, much genuine friendliness and kindness to be found among the native inhabitants of the pilgrim kingdom.

Pilgrimage can be undertaken alone, with one or two companions or in a larger organised group. It can be intentional, casual or random. More than other forms of travel, it involves a certain vulnerability in being open to others and to experiences that may be unsettling or disturbing as well as exhilarating and reassuring. In pilgrimage, the return journey is as important as the outward journey or the destination. The pilgrim comes back changed and hopefully more open as well as more faithful than before. The late eighteenth-century French writer Chateaubriand maintained that 'there was never a pilgrim that did not come back to his own village with one less prejudice and one more idea'.

Ultimately pilgrimages, especially those involving physical exertion, are like life itself. The Fife Pilgrim Way has its dull stretches along boring and uninteresting roads, through grim surroundings and past ugly buildings as well as offering moments of beauty and elation walking through woods and beside streams or contemplating a sunset over distant hills. Every pilgrimage has its own rhythms and rituals, its ebb and flow of arriving and departing, exodus and return. The outer physical journey mirrors the inner spiritual journey.

Before concluding this introduction, I want to acknowledge and pay tribute to those who have developed and walked other pilgrim ways through Fife over recent decades. Several pioneered routes before the Fife Pilgrim Way was conceived and planned. Perhaps the first in the field was Cameron Black, who researched a route from Edinburgh to St Andrews, which he called the St Andrew's Way, following more directly in the wake of medieval pilgrims via South and North Queensferry, Dunfermline, Keltybridge, Scotlandwell, Falkland, Kingskettle and Ceres. This was the route chosen in reverse for the Pilgrims Crossing Scotland 2000 project, part of the Europe-wide Christian celebrations to mark the dawn of the third millennium. Over four days in September 2000 a group of several hundred pilgrims walked from St Andrews to Edinburgh carrying a large oak cross. Their pilgrimage provided the western 'arm' of a huge cross which was traced by pilgrims walking across Europe, from Trondheim in Norway in the north, Thessaloniki in the south and Iaşi in Romania in the east. I was among those who set off on 10 September on the first leg to Ceres following a commissioning service in St Andrews Cathedral. The pilgrimage reached its destination, Holyrood Abbey, on 14 September, Holy Cross (or Holy Rood) Day, commemorating the occasion when King David, hunting in the forest below Arthur's Seat, saved himself from attack by brandishing the cross-shaped antlers of a stag and subsequently vowed to set up an abbey on the site in thanksgiving for his deliverance. On St Andrew's Day 2000 the cross which had been carried by the pilgrims was erected on Inchgarvie Island in the Forth, where it can still be clearly seen by those travelling across the Forth rail bridge.

There have been a number of recent Roman Catholic pilgrimages from North Queensferry to St Andrews. In 2011 Hugh Lockhart, a retired soldier, devised a route called The Way of St Andrews, and also known as St Margaret's Way, which uses the Fife coastal path until just before Earlsferry (the destination of a medieval pilgrim sea crossing from North Berwick) and then strikes north through Kilconquhar, Colinsburgh and Largoward to St Andrews. In August 2016 members of the Confraternity of Ninian, which is dedicated to the reconversion of Scotland to Roman Catholicism through pilgrimage, walked in three days from the shrine of St Andrew in St Mary's Roman Catholic Cathedral in Edinburgh via Dunfermline, Kelty, Scotlandwell, the Lomond hills, Falkland, Ladybank, Springfield, Cupar and Blebocraigs to St Andrews Cathedral, where they celebrated Mass in Latin as it would have been done before the Reformation. The 'Two Shrines Pilgrimage' as it is called has become an annual event. Those involved in a charismatic Roman Catholic group called 'New Dawn' make a much shorter pilgrimage through the streets of St Andrews every July and celebrate Mass (in English) in the cathedral ruins as part of their annual gathering in the town. There was a particularly memorable and moving celebration there on 5 July 2018, the 700th anniversary to the day of the cathedral's consecration, not least because of the seemingly miraculous appearance of a saltire formed by cloud vapour in the otherwise blue sky at the moment of consecration. It remained floating above the east end throughout the distribution of the elements and faded away at the end of the Mass.

There have been other notable projects to promote pilgrimage in Fife. The St Andrews Cathedral Project was founded in 2000 on the initiative of David Dow, an architect based in north-east Fife, with the aim of resurrecting St Andrews Cathedral as a pilgrim destination and to promote pilgrimage to people of all faiths and none. It mounted several temporary exhibitions on the theme of medieval pilgrimage through Fife in churches and other venues in and around St Andrews under the title 'Sair Hearts, Sair Feet, Sair Heads'. It also developed an interesting and fruitful inter-faith dimension by linking Christians with Muslims in Dundee. I was privileged to take part in a packed meeting in St Andrews in which both Muslims and Christians shared their own experience of pilgrimage.

Forth Pilgrim Ltd was set up as a Social Enterprise Company in 2007 by Roger and Eileen Pickering with the goal of establishing a 300-mile pilgrim way from St Andrews to Durham. They have grown interest by leading guided walks for groups to pilgrim places like Dunfermline and St Andrews. Through teaching the history of pilgrimage outdoors with school groups using drama, costume and fun, they engage young people in 'history where it happened'.

Roger Pickering's own enthusiasm was a major catalyst in the early development of the Fife Pilgrim Way and was instrumental in drawing various organisations and individuals who met round the table in 2012 into a lasting alliance.

Among several pilgrimage routes devised by Donald Smith of the Scottish Storytelling Centre in Edinburgh is the St Margaret Journey, which offers two routes from North Queensferry to St Andrews, one

using the Fife coast path and the other broadly taking the same course as Cameron Black's St Andrews Way. These routes were planned on the initiative of the Scottish Churches Trust and are promoted on the website 'Scottish Pilgrim Journeys', and in the *Pilgrim Guide to Scotland* (2015).

So, just as Jesus tells us that His Father's house has many mansions, there are many different ways of traversing the pilgrim kingdom of Fife. This book will focus on the officially designated, established and waymarked Fife Pilgrim Way, which means that it will not cover the significant historical and spiritual sites at Loch Leven, Scotlandwell (which is, in fact, in Kinross and outside the kingdom of Fife) and Falkland which were on the medieval pilgrim route. It is not a guide-book. It does not aim to provide detailed descriptions of buildings and sites along the way, although many are mentioned, nor is it designed to help modern pilgrims navigate their way. Rather, it aims to set the Fife Pilgrim Way in its historical and spiritual context. It tells the stories of those who have walked this way before – among them monks, miners and martyrs – because a key part of pilgrimage is following in other people's footsteps. It sketches in something of the traditions and history, especially the religious history, of the places and communities along the route. It also offers brief spiritual reflections and themes to ponder at the end of each section. You do not need to take it with you in your knapsack – it won't tell you where you have taken a wrong turning or help you when you need to find the nearest toilet or bus stop. It is more for reading before you set out and perhaps again after you return – or even indeed to help armchair pilgrims to make the journey in their imaginations. There are many ways to be a pilgrim and not all of them involve putting on walking boots or cycle clips and braving the elements. I hope that this book will enhance the appreciation and deepen the experience of those who journey on the Fife Pilgrim Way in whatever way they choose or are able.

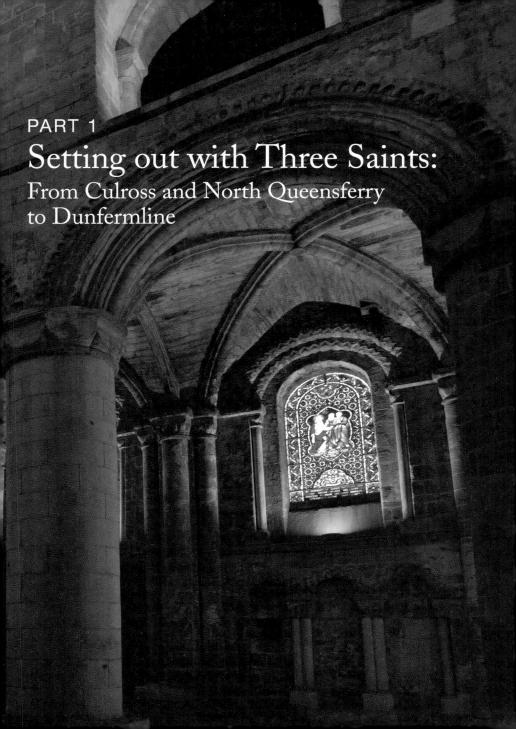

# PART 1
# Setting out with Three Saints:
## From Culross and North Queensferry to Dunfermline

# I
# Setting out from Culross with Serf and Kentigern

Although most medieval pilgrims began their journey to St Andrews from North Queensferry, and it may seem more logical for modern pilgrims to begin there as well, the alternative starting point of Culross offers two distinct advantages. First, as one of the most picturesque and perfectly preserved burgh towns in Scotland, it provides a more scenic and historical setting from which to begin the journey through Fife. Second, it allows pilgrims to set off in the company of two early Celtic saints, Serf and Kentigern.

Previous spread
Dunfermline
Abbey nave

Culross lies in the south-west corner of Fife. It only became part of the pilgrim kingdom in 1891, when it was transferred from Perthshire by the Boundary Commissioners. It reached the height of its prosperity in the late sixteenth and early seventeenth centuries when George Bruce, who is commemorated by an imposing memorial in a family vault attached to the parish church, exploited the rich coal seams under the Forth and also developed a successful salt manufacturing business. Extensive trade with the Low Countries and Scandinavia made its harbour the fourth biggest in Scotland. The picturesque houses that line the cobbled streets rising steeply from the shore (and called either causeways or braes) date from this period. Another important industry was the manufacture of iron girdle pans for making pancakes and oatcakes. These industries have long since gone and the small town fell into considerable decline until the newly formed National Trust for Scotland set about restoring its 'little houses' in the 1930s. It now has something of a picture-postcard appearance, but pilgrims setting off from here cannot but be conscious of the industrial landscape nearby. Looking out across the Forth, the skyline is dominated by the tanks, pipes and chimneys of the huge Grangemouth oil refinery opposite, and to the west stands the gaunt outline of the Longannet Power Station, the last coal-fired power station in Scotland, which was closed in 2016. Grangemouth has not been without its problems, and with the phasing-out of fossil fuels there must be a question mark over its future. This industrial landscape proves a salutary reminder of the temporary and transitory nature of human endeavour and industry as pilgrims begin their journey.

Long before it was an industrial and trading centre, Culross was important primarily for its religious associations and significance, and this is what also makes it such a good starting point for pilgrims. The town is dominated by the parish church, constructed out of the choir of the thirteenth-century Cistercian abbey and enhanced by an imposing early sixteenth-century tower, which, together with the abbey ruins,

Opposite
Culross Abbey

stands proudly at the top of a steep hill. A much earlier ecclesiastical settlement was associated with the figures of Serf and Kentigern. Their saintly companionship allows those embarking on the Fife Pilgrim Way to connect with the rich heritage of Celtic Christianity in its so-called golden age from the mid fifth to the late seventh centuries, and to revel in its legends, miracles and larger-than-life characters. Several other Celtic saints from this period have associations with Fife, albeit rather tentative ones in many cases – they will be briefly mentioned at the end of this chapter – but Culross has strong connections with these two particular saints, who stand alongside Ninian and Columba in the front rank of Scottish Christian leaders in the early Middle Ages.

What is written about Serf and Kentigern in the paragraphs that follow comes with a strong health warning. In common with most of their contemporaries they were the objects of hagiography – exaggerated, fanciful write-ups – to enhance their sanctity and the reputation of the ecclesiastical institutions with which they became associated, rather

than biography in the sense that we would understand it today. False news, spin and propaganda may seem characteristic features of our own times, but they were also much to the fore in the Middle Ages, not least among the monastic chroniclers who wrote up the lives of early saints, inventing stories and incidents to enhance the reputation of a particular monastery. Whereas Ninian and Columba were both written about close to their own lifetimes, the earliest extant accounts of the lives of Serf and Kentigern did not appear until 500 years or more after their deaths, and their historicity and factual accuracy must be regarded as very dubious. The earliest life of Serf, entitled *Vita Sancti Servani*, appears in a thirteenth-century Irish manuscript and was possibly written by a monk in the Cistercian abbey at Culross soon after its foundation in 1217, although it could conceivably have an earlier provenance. Early in the fifteenth century Andrew of Wyntoun, a canon of St Andrews who became Prior of St Serf's Priory on Loch Leven, composed a chronicle recording further stories about Serf. The first known Life of Kentigern was written by an anonymous author in the mid twelfth century for Bishop Herbert of Glasgow to boost the prestige and reputation of Glasgow Cathedral. The same purpose underlay a second Life, written later in the same century by Jocelin of Furness, a well-known monastic hagiographer.

There were almost certainly other earlier written sources telling stories about these two men, both of whom were ordained monks, and their saintly deeds and miracles were also made much of in later medieval liturgical works presenting readings, hymns and prayers for the commemoration of Scottish saints. The Sprouston Breviary of *c.* 1300 contains a rhymed office set to medieval plainchant for the feast of St Kentigern (13 January). It received its first complete performance in modern times from the group Capella Nova in a series of concerts in 1997, and can be heard on a CD recording. The Aberdeen Breviary of 1510, the most important collection that we have of Scottish saints' lives, contains lengthy readings to be used on the feast days of both saints (Serf is celebrated on 1 July). All of these sources present the two saints as exceptionally holy figures and give a clear sense of the cults that developed around them, and their significance in early medieval Scottish devotion and piety. What they do not provide is any sound historical evidence. We are in the realm here of pious veneration rather than historical research.

Serf was the earlier and more shadowy of the two saints associated with Culross. According to the *Vita Sancti Servana* he had exotic origins, being the son of the King of Canaan; he went to study divinity at Alexandria in Egypt, where he became a monk and a priest. Returning to Canaan, he was elected a bishop and after twenty years was called by an angel to go to Jerusalem, where he was immediately made a patriarch. He subsequently went to Constantinople and Rome, where he was elected Pope, an office he held for seven years. His wanderings then took him across the Alps and continental Europe until he finally reached the eastern shores of Scotland. He settled in the vicinity of the Ochil Hills, where he carried out missionary work and became well known for his austere devotion and faith. He also spent time in East Lothian, and one day threw his staff across the Forth from the vicinity of Kinneil, resolving to set up a church where it landed. It travelled far up and across the river estuary and finally landed on a promontory full of prickly thorn bushes, where it miraculously sprouted into a fruit tree. Serf and his followers duly set up their monastery at this place, which was known as Culross – in Gaelic *Cuileann Ros*, the holly point or promontory.

This wildly improbable story is, not surprisingly, discounted by all historians. It is more likely that Serf was a Gaelic, British or Pictish monk – the Aberdeen Breviary records that he came from the race of the Scots. He does seem to have had associations with the area around the Ochil Hills, and specifically the vicinity of Alva and Tillicoultry. There are also several stories which give him Fife connections. He is said to have turned water into wine at Dysart and also to have had a heated theological debate with the Devil in a cave there. Possibly this was a place of retreat for him – the name Dysart, found in various forms throughout Celtic Britain, indicates a desert place where monks went to be alone, following the example of the desert fathers of Egypt and Syria. He is also credited in several sources with founding a small monastery on the island in Loch Leven, which still bears his name. At least nine churches in Fife appear to have been dedicated to Serf during the Middle Ages.

Serf's principal monastic foundation seems to have been at Culross, which according to some accounts he was given as the site for a church by the Pictish King Brude IV, whom he had cured from a deadly illness. He appears to have set up a school for young boys there and, according to the *Vita Sancti Servani*, that was where he was buried, having died at Dunning, which was the site of another of his spectacular miracles, the slaying of a dragon. Certainly, Culross seems to have become the centre of the posthumous cult which grew up around Serf, possibly several hundred years after his death. The presence of his enshrined remains was probably what led the Cistercians to establish their monastery there in the early thirteenth century. There is only limited evidence of pilgrimages to Serf's shrine at Culross later in the Middle Ages, although there is mention in 1511 of James IV making an offering of fourteen shillings to St Serf's reliquary.

It is extremely difficult to date Serf with any degree of accuracy. The Aberdeen Breviary makes him a contemporary of Bishop Palladius, who was sent by the Pope to the Scots in the early fifth century. Mentions of him in the Lives of Kentigern would suggest that he lived in the later sixth century, but other sources make him a contemporary of Adomnán, the Abbot of Iona and biographer of Columba, who died around 700. This late dating would tie in with the reference to King Brude IV, who reigned between *c.* 697 and 706, giving him the land at Culross for his monastery. In the words of Alan MacQuarrie, the leading modern authority on the early Scottish saints, 'if one were to conflate all these accounts, St Serf would have a lifespan of over 300 years, surely a record for longevity even among Scottish saints' (Macquarrie 2012: 415). Those responsible for interpreting Culross' heritage today hedge their bets – the display in the south transept of the abbey church puts him confidently in the sixth century, whereas the National Trust for Scotland interpretation board outside by the abbey ruins opts for the early eighth century. It is all frustratingly (or delightfully, depending on your perspective) vague and fluid.

We are on slightly surer ground when it comes to Kentigern, although there is also much that is similarly improbable in the stories relating to his origins. According to both the twelfth-century lives, he was the illegitimate child of Enoch, or Thenew, the Christian daughter of Loth, a pagan king of Lothian. One version of the story recounts that she was violently raped by the son of the King of Cumbria dressed as a woman. The shame of this incident caused her father to banish her. He ordered her to be taken to the top of a high hill in a carriage and thrown down from it to her death. Her prayers to God for deliverance were answered and when she landed on the ground she did not have a single bruise. Her father then put her in a boat and cast her off into a particularly rough sea – one of the Lives suggests that this may have happened at Aberlady on the north coast of East Lothian. The boat drifted across and up the Forth, passing the Isle of May and eventually landing at Culross. Enoch, who according to another source had conceived immaculately and without sexual intercourse in imitation of the Virgin Mary, to whom she was devoted, crawled up the shore and gave birth to a son while drying out by a fire which had been lit by shepherds. The shepherds subsequently took mother and baby to Serf, who blessed them and took them in to live with him. Serf called the child Kentigern, a name which is Brythonic (the language spoken through much of mainland Britain and the antecedent of modern Welsh) in origin, and he later also acquired the nickname Mungo, possibly derived from the Brythonic word 'mwyn', meaning gentle or kind.

Somewhat surprisingly, the *Vita Sancti Servani* does not mention Kentigern. Jocelin's Life of Kentigern, by contrast, suggests that the young Kentigern became Serf's star pupil and proved his sanctity by performing several miracles. His first one was to restore to life a robin who frequently entered Serf's cell and was regularly fed by him. One day some of the other boys whom Serf taught played roughly with the bird and pulled its head off. Kentigern, whom they blamed for this, put the head back on the robin's body, made the sign of the cross, prayed and restored it to life. His second miracle involved breathing over a hazel branch, which caught fire, enabling the relighting of the church lamps, which had been extinguished by his fellow pupils. He then moved up a league in the sanctity stakes by raising from the dead the cook who served Serf's monastic school. A common theme in all these miracle stories is Kentigern's unpopularity with his contemporaries, presumably because he was very much the favourite as well as the most saintly of the old man's pupils. Perhaps not surprisingly, he vowed to leave Culross, although Serf did not want him to go. The young monk fled the monastery with the waters of the Forth miraculously parting so that he could make his escape. They immediately closed in again, preventing the distraught Serf from following him.

According to the story as it is recounted in the twelfth-century Lives, Kentigern travelled westwards from Culross and eventually came to Glasgow, where he set up a church and subsequently became a bishop. He became credited with establishing Christianity in Strathclyde and is, of course, the patron saint of Glasgow. He also seems to have spent considerable periods of his later life evangelising in Cumbria and Wales. Jocelin's life describes him as visiting Rome several times and becoming a bishop as well as meeting with both St David and St Columba. We can be reasonably certain that the date of his death was around 612, as it is independently attested in early Welsh annals. Rather less likely is Jocelin's assertion that he lived until the age of 180 (although, if true, it would mean that he would have been born about the time Palladius came to Scotland in the early 430s and might be taken to support an early dating for Serf). His remains were enshrined at Glasgow, where they remain to this day in the crypt of the mighty cathedral which was built to house them and is dedicated to him. Unlike Serf, Kentigern/Mungo had no churches in Fife dedicated to him during the medieval period.

There is little, if anything, surviving now in Culross from the time of Serf and Kentigern. Those making the steep climb up to the abbey ruins will pass about halfway up on the wall of Erskine Brae the Lockit

Well, once the town's main water supply but now disused. A notice above it records that it was reputedly used 'by followers of St Serf' but this may be a little imaginative speculation, I fancy. There is no sign at all in the abbey church (nor is there any record) of Serf's shrine. There is a rather romantic little chapel built onto the east end of the church, which is now ruined and covered in green creepers – it is actually an early nineteenth-century Gothic burial enclosure. The only memorial to Serf and Kentigern is the east window of the church, which dates from 1905 and shows the two saints on either side of the Virgin Mary; John Gifford in the *Buildings of Scotland* guide to Fife describes it as 'soppy but colourful'.

Among the artefacts which are piled up in a slightly higgledy-piggledy fashion in the south aisle of the church is the base of a huge cross and some worn fragments of a cross shaft with characteristic Celtic knotwork. They are described on a nearby notice as being eighth or ninth century, but archaeologists are more inclined to date them to the tenth century. Whatever their date, they do suggest a considerable ecclesiastical settlement of some importance long before the coming of the Cistercians. Evidence from Loch Leven charters also suggests that there was a church at Culross in existence by the mid tenth century.

Kentigern is commemorated in a chapel between the abbey and the shore which was built in 1503 on the orders of Robert Blackadder, Bishop of St Andrews. There is not much of it left and it provides a rather underwhelming introduction to Culross's spiritual history to those coming into the town along the Low Causeway – the main route in from Dunfermline and the east. All that remains now are the lower parts of the walls, the altar at the east end, and the base of the rood screen which would have separated the chancel and the nave. These were discovered during an excavation in 1926, the chapel having presumably been demolished after the Reformation. It is rather dingy and understated today, with just a little notice attached to the back (north) wall bearing the name 'St Mungo's Chapel'. There is a sugges- tion that Blackadder sited the chapel where Kentigern was supposed to have been born – and this is possible, given that the tide and the

Overleaf Serf and Kentigern in east window, Culross Abbey

41

shoreline have retreated considerably over the centuries. A rather more imposing monument to the saint is provided by the smart nineteenth-century villa a few hundred yards along Low Causeway with the name 'St Kentigern' over its doorway.

If modern pilgrims cannot gain a great sense of the early presence of these two Celtic saints, there is much surviving from the later history of Culross to provide food for spiritual reflection and sustenance. The abbey ruins are evocative. The church was rebuilt in 1905–6 in a style that John Gifford rather delightfully describes as 'polite High Presbyterian' (Gifford 1988: 146). It may even perhaps be possible for future pilgrims to stay in one of the buildings formed out of the old abbey ruins. A charity entitled Support Culross Abbey Regeneration Trust (SCART for short) has been set up to raise money to buy the old manse, built in 1637 on the edge of the old cloisters and incorporating in its garden remains of both the cloisters and the lay brothers' refectory, with the aim of developing it as a community library and hostel for pilgrims walking the Fife Pilgrim Way.

Opposite
The Study,
Culross

If they have time before setting out, pilgrims would be well advised to take one of the excellent National Trust tours which run on the hour in the afternoon between late March and late October. These involve walking up the steep brae to the Mercat Cross, surmounted by the unicorn, the national animal of Scotland. Overlooking it on one side is a pink-harled seventeenth-century house with a Greek motto inscribed on the lintel over the front window that translates as 'God provides and will provide' – a reassuring text for pilgrims setting out. On the other side of the road an outside staircase leads to a house that was long known as 'The Nunnery' but was, in fact, a brothel. The tour also gives access to the interiors of two of the town's most interesting buildings: the tiny room in the gabled tower known as The Study where Robert Leighton, the unusually ecumenically minded and eirenic mid seventeenth-century Bishop of Dunblane, who had a house in the town, was wont to retire to practise his sermons; and the court room in the Town House where numerous witchcraft trials were held. Those found guilty of witchcraft were imprisoned in the tower

of this building; there is also a local tradition that witches were imprisoned in the tower of the abbey. Visiting these two atmospheric buildings points up two contrasting aspects of Scotland's post-Reformation religious history – the bigotry and prejudice which led so many women to be put to death as witches, often simply on the basis of physical deformities or personality quirks, and the liberal, broad-minded spirit of divines like Leighton, who sought to bring some moderation and tolerance into the country's bitterly divided religious life.

Serf and Kentigern are not the only early Christian saints we will encounter along the Fife Pilgrim Way. Others commemorated in church dedications include Drostan at Markinch and Kenneth at Kennoway. Such dedications cannot be taken as proof that these individuals ever had a close connection with or even visited the places concerned. The great majority of church dedications in Fife are from the twelfth century onwards and do not necessarily imply a physical link with a person who died 500 or so years earlier. The saints associated with medieval Fife were a motley lot, ranging from kings and queens, virgins and martyrs, bishops and abbots to hermits and confessors. Giles Dove has identified and enumerated around seventy of them in his interesting thesis (Dove 1988). However uncertain their actual association with the places where they were commemorated, they were a real spiritual presence. The cult of saints in the Middle Ages was brought about by a mixture of hero worship, the need for protection and a fascination with fanciful legends and stories. Saints fulfilled similar roles to pop stars and footballers today as iconic figures who were both role models and somewhat exotic celebrities. Their miracles and protection could be invoked to heal ills and ward off danger, and their intercessions harnessed in the ever urgent and pressing business of securing salvation and avoiding the fiery furnaces of Hell.

If we are to understand the appeal of these saints we need to remember how limited the reading and knowledge of many people was in the Middle Ages. Their devotion was centred on the Bible and it is not surprising that many of the stories about saints, and notably about their miracles, seem to have been lifted directly from Gospel stories about Jesus. This is true of other aspects of their lives – the account of the shepherds discovering the infant Kentigern in Jocelin's Life, for example, is an almost direct paraphrase of Luke's account of the shepherds in Jesus' nativity story. These biblical sources were mixed with other elements that often seem to owe more to pagan magic and pre-Christian folklore, such as the story that despite being worn for long hours in the rain and snow, Kentigern's garments remained completely dry. Such apparent conjuring tricks were coupled with accounts of the saints' austere asceticism. Kentigern is portrayed in the Aberdeen Breviary as reciting the entire Psalter while sitting on a stone in cold running water. This intriguing mixture of tall and edifying stories makes the saints both appealing and somewhat daunting companions along the pilgrim way.

The practice of naming churches in Fife after Celtic saints has continued until the present day. Two of the Church of Scotland churches built in the new town of Glenrothes were dedicated respectively to St Columba (1960) and St Ninian (1970). For these hardy Christian pioneers pilgrimage, or *peregrinatio* as they called it, was not about travelling to holy places or venerating relics to get a spiritual high but rather a state of costly perpetual exile from comforts, distractions and pleasures to live as they believed Jesus had lived, and to witness to Him through austere, dedicated lives. They present a tough and challenging model for modern pilgrims to follow.

There is, of course, one outstanding Scottish saint who stands alongside Andrew as joint patron of the nation and who has not yet been mentioned. For those starting from North Queensferry she is a constant companion along the Fife Pilgrim Way, and the Culross pilgrims meet her at Dunfermline. It is time to set out with Margaret.

## 2

# Setting out from North Queensferry with Margaret

The alternative starting point for the Fife Pilgrim Way, North Queensferry, immediately introduces pilgrims to the person who did more than anyone else to make Fife the pilgrim kingdom, Queen Margaret. The first woman to take a prominent role in the religious life of Scotland and the only medieval Scottish saint to be officially canonised, she is widely regarded as Scotland's second patron saint and arguably has a much stronger claim than Andrew to be the nation's protector and spiritual guide.

Queen Margaret's imprint is unmistakable and unavoidable in North Queensferry, most obviously, of course, in the name of this small settlement on the north shore of the Forth, which owes its existence to the fact that she chose it in the late eleventh century as the landing place for the ferry bringing pilgrims bound for St Andrews from the similarly named South Queensferry on the other side of the estuary. Margaret provided not just the ferry crossing but also hostels for pilgrims on either side, and more besides as her chaplain and biographer, Turgot, described:

Since the church of St Andrews was frequented by the devout who flocked to it from all quarters, she erected dwellings on either shore of the sea which divides Lothian from Scotland, so that pilgrims and poor people might shelter there and rest themselves after the fatigues of their journey. She had arranged they should find there all that they needed for the refreshment of the body. Servants were appointed, whose special duty it was to see that everything which might be required for these wayfarers should be always in readiness, and who were directed to attend upon them with all diligence. Moreover, she provided ships for the transport of these pilgrims both coming and going, nor was it lawful to demand any fee for the passage from those who were crossing (Turgot 1896: 59–60).

The significance of this particular ferry crossing across the Forth was considerable. It was seen by many as giving access to the proper Scotland, the land north of the Forth–Clyde line and known as Alba, which had been forged by the uniting of Pictland and Dalriada, the western kingdom of the Gaels. Lothian was for long a part of the Anglo-Saxon kingdom of Northumbria and it is noticeable how Turgot distinguished it from Scotland on the other side of the Forth. As late as the 1720s Daniel Defoe wrote prior to crossing into Fife, 'I am now to enter the real and true Caledonia, for the country north of the firth is alone called by that name' (Fawcett 2005: 102). Margaret chose the location for her crossing wisely – it was more protected than crossings further out into the sea like the one between North Berwick and Earlsferry which was also used by medieval pilgrims to St Andrews, and it had the advantage of the 'stepping stone' of Inchgarvie Island, offering shelter if the sea suddenly turned rough. The crossing which she established seems originally to have been known as *Passagium de Inverkeithin* and appears only to have taken the name *Ad Portum Reginae* after 1129, when it was granted to the abbot and monks of Dunfermline by King David I with the stipulation that all pilgrims should have free passage. The ferry rights were confirmed by subsequent monarchs and when it became too much for the monks to manage, the ferry franchise was given to 'substantial seamen' who were allowed to levy a charge. In the nineteenth century the ferry was vested in trustees. The first steamboat put into service on the crossing in 1821 was named *Queen Margaret*, and this name was also used for one of the diesel electric paddle-driven boats built in 1934 which carried passengers and cars across the Forth until the ferry service stopped with the building of the first road bridge in 1964. The replacement bridge, opened in 2017, is known as the Queensferry Crossing.

There is little now remaining of the old pilgrim ferry terminal at North Queensferry. The old jetty provides a good place from which to view the two road bridges and also the mighty rail bridge, constructed between 1883 and 1890, which towers above. Tucked away in the aptly named Chapel Place a couple of streets back from the waterfront are the ruins of a chapel dedicated to St James, the traditional protector of pilgrims, and first mentioned in a document of around 1320 in which it is granted by King Robert I and William Lamberton, Bishop of St Andrews, to the monks of Dunfermline Abbey, on condition that they provided two chaplains for the chapel, repaired and preserved it, and furnished it with a chalice, vestments and books. It was perhaps the first port of call for pilgrims keen to give thanks after making a safe passage across the Forth. Severe damage was apparently done to the chapel by Oliver Cromwell's troops in 1651 and all that now remains are parts of the walls and a sixteenth-century mullioned window in the west gable. In the mid eighteenth century a graveyard was established within the old chapel walls by the North Queensferry Sailors' Society. A roughly carved stone plaque by the locked entrance gate reads: 'This is done by sailers [*sic*] in North Ferrie, 1752'. One of the sailors' graves has the moving inscription (rendered here in modern English):

Now here we lay at anchor
With many in our fleet,
In hopes to weigh at the last day
Our Admiral Christ to meet

Margaret has also given her name to the small settlement of St Margaret's Hope which lies just up the shore from North Queensferry, almost directly under the northern end of the Queensferry crossing

Opposite
St James'
Chapel, North
Queensferry

THIS IS DONE BY
THE SAILERS IN
NORTH FERRIE·
17                5 2

next to a boggy area known as St Margaret's Marsh. This is where tradition has it that she first landed when she came to Scotland in or around 1067. It is significant that she came to Fife not as a pilgrim but rather as a refugee and an exile. Like so many women down the ages, her travels were occasioned by necessity and the urgent imperative to flee violence and danger rather than by a conscious desire for pilgrimage.

Margaret's ancestry lay in the Anglo-Saxon royal line. Her grandfather, Edmund II, was King of England for less than a year in 1016 before being murdered when the throne was seized by the Danish Canute. His son Edward Aetheling went into exile first in Sweden and then in southern Hungary. Known as Edward the Exile, he married Agatha, a German or Hungarian princess, in 1043 and their daughter Margaret was born in Hungary two or three years later. In 1056, Edward was called back to England by his uncle Edward the Confessor as heir apparent to the throne, but he died soon after arriving. Agatha and her three children, Margaret, Edgar and Christina, remained in the English court until their safety became compromised when William the Conqueror took the throne after the Battle of Hastings in 1066. They were advised to flee to Scotland and made the perilous sea crossing there. Some stories suggest that they were driven ashore in a storm at the place which later became known as St Margaret's Hope – one version even has it that they were trying to return to Hungary – but it seems much more likely that this was their intended landing place and that they had been invited to seek refuge in Fife by King Malcolm III, who had ruled Scotland since 1058 and had his main base in Dunfermline.

According to tradition, Agatha and her three children walked from their landing place to Dunfermline via Inverkeithing. They are said to have rested on the journey at the large slab of sandstone known as St Margaret's Stone which is now sited somewhat incongruously in front of a large office block belonging to Lloyds Bank, beside the entrance to Pitreavie Business Park just off the very busy B980 Queensferry Road between Rosyth and Dunfermline, having been moved from its original location nearby to allow for road-building. Other stories suggest that Margaret sat on or by this stone when queen to make herself available to anyone who wished to consult her. Another version of the story of her arrival in Scotland has it that the family party of exiles was met at their landing place by Malcolm III. This provided the inspiration for William Hole's painting, now in the Scottish National Portrait Gallery, showing the king tenderly greeting the attractive princess, twenty years younger than him, who was later to become his wife.

Malcolm had a somewhat similar background to Margaret, having himself been forced to go into exile as a boy when his father, King Duncan I, was killed by Macbeth. Malcolm was sent to the court of Edward the Confessor in England and stayed there for fourteen years. It is likely that he got to know Margaret and her family as fellow exiles at the English court in 1056. He returned to Scotland later that year, defeated and killed Macbeth in 1057, and after killing Macbeth's stepson, Lulach, was crowned King of Scots in 1058. He moved the main residence of the Scottish court from Forteviot in Perthshire to Dunfermline, possibly establishing his primitive palace in the well-fortified building known as Malcolm's Tower in what is now Pittencrieff Park around 1065, although there is some doubt about this and the first royal residence may have been on the site of the later medieval palace near the abbey. Known as Canmore (*Ceann Mór*, Gaelic for the great chieftain), he was a fierce warrior and a sworn enemy of the Normans, but also generous and kind. A strong friend and champion of the Anglo-Saxon royal house, it was probably he who persuaded Agatha and her children to come north to Scotland and find sanctuary in his court.

Malcolm, whose first wife, Ingibjörg, the daughter of the Norse earl of Orkney, seems to have died around 1068, was extremely keen to marry Margaret. He was undoubtedly taken by her beauty and innocence but was also enthusiastic about the match for dynastic reasons in order to unite the Saxon heirs to the English throne with the Scottish royal family. She was initially reluctant, having vowed to

53

spend her life as a nun, but he won her over and they were married in Dunfermline in or around 1069 in what was the first real union of the crowns of England and Scotland. It is not entirely clear where the marriage took place – possibly in Malcolm's Tower, or perhaps in the small church which stood on the site of what would later become Dunfermline Abbey. The marriage was portrayed as the union of beauty and the beast and Margaret seems to have taken on Malcolm as something of a challenge and a religious duty, in order to instruct him in the Christian faith and be in a position to encourage Christianity throughout his kingdom. In both aims she succeeded. According to Turgot, 'by the help of God she instructed her husband in the works of justice, mercy, almsgiving and other virtues'. An idealised late nineteenth-century portrait by Sir Joseph Noel Paton showing her engaged in this activity hangs in the entrance to Dunfermline City Chambers. Turgot claimed that she also had a profound effect on Malcolm's spiritual life: 'from her he learned how to keep the vigils of the night in constant prayer; she instructed him by her exhortation and example how to pray to God with groaning from the heart and abundance of tears' (Turgot 1896: 39).

Margaret's contribution to the Church both in Fife and across Scotland was enormous. With her husband's support, she established a new, larger church in Dunfermline, dedicated to the Holy Trinity and staffed by Benedictine monks brought up from Canterbury. As well as assisting pilgrims to St Andrews with the ferry crossing and hospices, she gave a magnificent crucifix for the shrine of St Andrew and may have initiated and supported the building of St Rule's Church to house his relics.

As a girl living in Hungary, Margaret had been much influenced by the profoundly religious atmosphere in the court of King Stephen, Hungary's patron saint and first Christian king. Her religious upbringing continued during her teenage years at the court of Edward the Confessor, the saintly founder of Westminster Abbey. Her sister, Christina, spent much of her adult life as a nun and Margaret initially intended to pursue the same vocation. Even in her married state, with six children, she spent much of every day in personal devotions. The English Benedictine monk Turgot, whom she took on as personal chaplain and counsellor, wrote a hagiographical Life after her death which portrayed her as deeply pious, giving away much money to the poor and always serving orphans and other poor people with food before she herself ate. Indeed, Turgot criticised her for eating so sparingly and regularly starving herself – she fasted for forty days before Christmas as well as through Lent – leading to chronic stomach pains throughout her life. She was strict with her children and brought them up to be God-fearing Christians. Overall, in the words of Professor Robert Bartlett of St Andrews University, she emerges from Turgot's biography as 'an active and determined Christian lady' (Bartlett 2003: xxx).

Turgot gives a detailed account of the way in which Margaret habitually spent the forty days before Christmas and the entire season of Lent. She would sleep for a few hours early in the night and then rise to say all the night offices before returning to her chamber to wash the feet of six poor people. After another brief sleep, she would spend much of the morning in prayer and reading the psalms, and ordered that nine destitute little orphans be brought to her to have food and comfort. Later, 300 poor people would be admitted to the royal hall where the king and queen would serve them with food and drink and give them alms. The queen would then return to the church for lengthy prayers and to recite the Psalter before partaking of Mass. Before taking her own evening meal – her only food of the day – she would personally wait on twenty-four poor people, whom she insisted should always be living in close proximity to her wherever she was. Her own meal – frugal and scanty – 'rather excited hunger than allayed it. She seemed to taste of food, not to take it' (Turgot 1896: 64).

Margaret is often portrayed as having destroyed the old Celtic or Culdee Christian church in Scotland and replaced it with more authoritarian and alien Roman practices. It is true that she sought to regularise liturgical practices, including the observance of Lent and the use of Latin rather than Gaelic in worship, and that she signalled her support

Margaret and Malcolm
as portrayed by
Sir Joseph Noel Paton

for the continental religious orders by bringing Benedictine monks to Dunfermline. She also greatly increased the formality and ceremonial of court life and etiquette as well as its piety, enforcing strict observance of the Sabbath, with no manual labour being allowed. Turgot described how she greatly increased the ritual, splendour and spectacle of the court and how she also enriched the worship of the Church with ornaments and vestments: 'Her chamber was never without such objects, those I mean which appertained to the dignity of the divine service. It was, so to speak, a workshop of sacred art: in which copes for the cantors, chasubles, stoles, altar-cloths, together with other priestly vestments and church ornaments of an admirable beauty, were always to be seen, either already made, or in course of preparation' (Turgot 1896: 30).

It would, however, be wrong to see Margaret, as she is sometimes portrayed, as the destroyer of the old so-called Celtic Church and its ways. Her own austere ascetic practices and profound piety and devotion stood very much in the tradition of Celtic Christianity and the monasticism practised by Serf and Mungo. Turgot noted that she took a particular interest in and strongly supported the many Christian anchorites and hermits leading solitary lives of prayer around Scotland. She also took an interest in the monastic community on Iona which Columba had founded 500 years earlier. She seems to have supported the small group of monks on the island and there is a tradition that she sponsored the construction of the earliest stone building on Iona, St Oran's Chapel, although this is unlikely. She went on several pilgrimages herself and was a keen devotee of the cult of relics, possessing a casket containing what she believed to be a piece of Christ's cross. Probably acquired in Hungary, it became known as the Black Rood of Scotland. She also had a Gospel book which, according to Turgot, fell into a stream but did not get wet. This book disappeared for a long time. In 1887 a Gospel book bought in auction by the Bodleian Library, Oxford, was found to have a Latin prayer written inside describing this miracle and it is thought that it may well be the one that Turgot mentioned and Margaret owned.

Both Malcolm and Margaret died in 1093 and were buried in the Church of the Holy Trinity which they had founded in Dunfermline. With three of their sons, Edgar, Alexander I and David, becoming kings of Scotland, they established a formidable royal dynasty that was to rule Scotland for nearly 200 years, bringing it peace and prosperity.

Before setting off from North Queensferry along the pilgrim way, it is worth casting a further lingering glance back to the notoriously rough sea around this little peninsula. It played a key role in the lives, and deaths, of several of Margaret and Malcolm's royal successors as they tried to cross the Forth. In 1123 their son Alexander I was caught in a fierce storm which blew him onto the island of Inchcolm. After safely landing there, he founded a monastery, the ruins of which can still be seen on the island, in gratitude for his safe deliverance. In 1153 the body of his successor, David I, who had died at Carlisle Castle, was being carried back for burial at Dunfermline Abbey. The waters of the Forth were so choppy that there was great hesitation about entrusting his coffin to a boat. After much prayer, the funeral party decided to make the crossing. As soon as they had placed the royal corpse on the boat the storm subsided, only to rise up again after they had landed safely on the north shore. The last of the dynasty established by Margaret and Malcolm Canmore, King Alexander III, also made a landing on the Fife coast near North Queensferry but in his case it was with tragic consequences. On 18 March 1286 he set out from Edinburgh to Fife to visit his queen, Yolande of Dreux, who was residing at Kinghorn, because it was her birthday the following day. Despite being warned not to cross the Forth because of atrocious weather conditions, he insisted on setting off and eventually made a landing from the storm near where Margaret had landed more than 200 years earlier. He became separated from his guides and in the dark his horse seems to have lost its footing. The forty-four year-old king was found dead on the shore of the beach at Pettycur Bay between Burntisland and Kinghorn the following morning with a broken neck, his horse having apparently fallen over a rocky embankment.

It is a strange coincidence that the last of the dynasty, sometimes referred to as the Celtic line and sometimes the House of Dunkeld, or even the 'Margaretsons', which had provided Scottish monarchs for around 200 years, should have come to grief near where its founder, Margaret, had first stepped ashore. Alexander III had no obvious male heir and his death ushered in a period of dynastic uncertainty and political conflict. His granddaughter and heiress, Margaret, Maid of Norway, set out from Norway to assume the Scottish crown at the age of seven in 1290, but she died on the way. This time it was not the waters of the Forth that were to blame – she took ill and died off the coast of Orkney. Into the power vacuum thus created came the English King Edward I, who spent some time in the royal palace at Dunfermline, his attempt to claim the Crown of Scotland leading to the so-called Wars of Independence and a lengthy period of unrest, instability and faction fighting.

We will return to Margaret when we reach Dunfermline, where she is naturally especially commemorated and remembered. She remains a continuing presence along the whole of the Fife Pilgrim Way, which she did so much to create and support. One of the Church of Scotland parish churches in Glenrothes is dedicated to her and she is the subject of a fine window in St James' Roman Catholic Church in St Andrews. It is good to see this recognition across the denominational spectrum of someone who remains an inspirational figure for her Christian charity, devotion and humility.

Opposite
St Margaret window, St James's Church, St Andrews

3
# Inverkeithing: a staging post and changing place

The short walk from North Queensferry to Inverkeithing, which follows the route of the Fife Coastal Path and can easily be accomplished in around an hour, provides a mini-pilgrimage in itself, with constantly changing scenery and opportunities to reflect on the theme of sacrifice and the impermanence of all human creations. It begins by ducking under one of the huge arches of the mighty Forth Railway Bridge and following a brick road over cliffs and through a wildlife reserve. There are fine views back over the Forth and in spring a profusion of bluebells and yellow gorse flowers. The path then dips down to run alongside the waters of the Forth. On this stretch there is a plaque recalling that 'near this spot on 20 June 1916 Lt. George Paton, 9th Battalion, Royal Scottish Fusiliers, aged 21, gave his life to save his men when a grenade was badly thrown'. The Fife Pilgrim Way next skirts the vast Inverkeithing Scrap Terminal, home of Robertson Metals Recycling, Shipbreakers, Scrap Metal Processors and Exporters, where huge forklift trucks load the crushed remains of cars and other once valuable items onto ships. As I walked past the terminal gates, and narrowly avoided being run down by one of the trucks coming out, I found myself pondering the fragility and impermanence of human life and the mysterious circle of life whereby death leads to regeneration and new birth.

Inverkeithing itself is reached by a long pull up Hope Street past St Peter's Episcopal Church and the modern Roman Catholic Church dedicated to St Peter in chains. It is not the most beautiful place on the Fife Pilgrim Way – in 1758 Sir William Burrell found it 'a mean, miserable, paultry town' – nor has it had the happiest history. The industries which once provided substantial local employment, based around shipbuilding, paper making and coal mining, are no more and today Inverkeithing is largely a dormitory town. It does, however, have a proud and significant past as a royal burgh and an important resting place and staging post for pilgrims. The earliest mention of a pilgrim hospital, or hostel, in Inverkeithing comes in a papal bull of 1196 confirming it as being among the possessions of the Abbey of Dryburgh. Some time later the Franciscans established a friary with a *hospitium* (guest house) attached to cater for the growing number of pilgrims passing through the town on their way to St Andrews. Local tradition suggests that the Dominicans, or Black Friars, established a house in Townhall Street known as The Priory which also took in pilgrims.

Inverkeithing first appears in a foundation charter for Scone Abbey granted by Alexander I and dated 1114 where it features alongside Edinburgh, Stirling, Perth and Aberdeen. The town was given burgh status in the twelfth century. The town had a long and close connection with royalty, partly because of its proximity to Dunfermline. There is a local tradition that David I built a royal palace there. Several medieval Scottish monarchs spent some time in the town and it was a favourite residence of Queen Anabella, consort of Robert III who reigned from 1390 to 1406. A convention of royal burghs was held there in 1487 and Inverkeithing continued to be visited by Scottish monarchs through the sixteenth and seventeenth centuries. Eighteenth-century visitors described a walled town with gates, rather like St Andrews. Reminders of its former glories can still be seen among the somewhat drab buildings in its High Street – there is a fine mercat cross dating from around 1400 and interesting architectural features include a lintel on the south wall of the former Providence House, now an optometrists, with the carved inscription 'God's Providence is My Inheritance – 1688'.

Local tradition suggests that Christianity was brought to this area in the late fifth century by St Erat, a follower of Ninian of Galloway, who is said to have preached by a well on a grassy hillside where the present church now stands. He is credited with founding the first place of worship on the site, which would have been a simple wattle and daub hut. This is a very early dating for the coming of Christianity to the east of Scotland, and no references to Erat exist in any medieval documents. He seems likely to have been a figure of legend rather than history. The first definite evidence of a church in Inverkeithing is provided by twelfth-century charters and papal bulls which describe it as being dedicated to St Peter and bequeathed to Dunfermline Abbey. The medieval parish church, probably built on the site of the earlier place of worship, stood, like its present-day successor, in a large churchyard on the east side of the main street through the town, now known as Church Street. It seems originally to have been a Norman building which was substantially rebuilt in Gothic style in the thirteenth century and consecrated to St Peter by Bishop David de Bernham, Bishop of St Andrews, in 1244. One of the few subsequent medieval references to it, dating from 1282, castigates the parish priest for inciting several young girls to dance in the churchyard in honour of 'Father Bacchus'. He was later found stabbed to death in the churchyard in what this document describes as 'divine retribution'. The church was substantially rebuilt in the fourteenth century with the addition of an imposing tower which still stands today. As well as the high altar, there were at least eight side altars, each with a chaplain endowed in the fifteenth and early sixteenth centuries by wealthy and royal patrons to say daily masses for their own souls and those of their ancestors. These were dedicated respectively to the Holy Blood, the Holy Rood, the Virgin Mary, Michael the Archangel, John the Baptist, Katherine of Alexandria, Laurence the Martyr and Ninian.

All these altars were destroyed along with other furnishings at the Reformation and the church was altered to make it much simpler and plainer. A heavy corbelled parapet was added to the tower in the sixteenth century and a squat lead-covered spire built in 1835. The main part of the modern church is a large, plain Perpendicular 'preaching

Opposite
Inverkeithing
Church

box' built after the rest of the building had been destroyed in 1825 by a fire caused by a spark from a brazier left unattended while plumbers working on the lead roof had lunch. It does not seem to have been a great loss – an architect's report in 1805 noted that 'the church has more the appearance of a cellar than a place of worship'. Another somewhat disparaging reference from the same period provides an account of the goings-on during the occasional all-day communion services, which began at 11 a.m. and lasted until 7 p.m. Worshippers periodically left the church and the overflow tent in the churchyard for refreshments, with young couples pairing off and a good deal of alcohol being consumed during what was supposed to be a solemn time of abstinence and devotion.

The interior of Inverkeithing parish church, which was refashioned in 1900 by the Scoto-Catholic architect Peter Macgregor Chalmers, contains some fine stained-glass windows, including one designed by Christian Shaw and installed in 1998 to mark the 750th anniversary of the church's consecration, which depicts various characters and episodes in its history, including Erat standing in front of the original wattle and daub hut and the building engulfed in flames in 1825. It also contains one of the finest medieval furnishings to survive in any Scottish parish church, a large, well-preserved, grey sandstone font of *c.* 1398, the bowl of which was discovered in 1806 buried in straw under the floor of the tower, having presumably been hidden there at the time of the Reformation. Nearby was a collection of bones, presumably the relics of a saint, which had been similarly buried at the same time. The pedestal base of the font had been lying in the churchyard without anyone realising what it was. With the discovery of the bowl, the font was reassembled and now stands prominently to the left of the communion table. Its six sides are decorated with sculptured angels holding armorial shields depicting, among others, the royal arms of Scotland and the coat of arms of the family of Queen Anabella. It is believed that the font was gifted to the church by King Robert III and Queen Anabella for the baptism of their first son, David, Earl of Carrick and later Duke of Rothesay. His dukedom was the first created in Scotland

and the title is still adopted by the heir apparent to the British throne when in Scotland.

The most important building in Inverkeithing from the point of view of pilgrims is the large *hospitium* or guesthouse of the Franciscan friary, also known as Greyfriars Convent, which stands prominently at the southern end of the High Street next to the modern Inverkeithing Centre (a useful resource providing a library, information centre, café and the all-important toilets so essential to comfortable pilgrimage). The friary may be late thirteenth century in origin. The erection and endowment of a church and convent for the Friars Minor at Inverkeithing is mentioned in a charter of 1268, but there are no further mentions of the friary until 1384/5. In its heyday the friary was a substantial building with living accommodation, chapel, cloisters and cellars occupying the area of what are now public gardens behind the *hospitium*. Foundations of the old north range and cellars can be seen in the gardens, as can a well which has been cleared and protected with an iron grille in the former courtyard. In 1559 the friary was dissolved and sold to John Swinton, who probably reconstructed the guesthouse and used the rest of the buildings as a quarry. The *hospitium* formed the west end of the friary. It has been much altered over the years, notably in the seventeenth century, but its massive walls and vaulted chambers still bear ample evidence of its medieval construction. The basement still houses the large arched passage, now bricked up, which formed the entrance to the friary.

Even in its reduced state, the *hospitium* in Inverkeithing constitutes the most substantial remains of a medieval friary in Scotland. It was at the heart of the friars' ministry of hospitality and must have been used as a stopping-off place by many pilgrims on their way either to St Andrews or Dunfermline. After a long period when it was used as the local library and then for other community purposes, there are now hopes of restoring it as a modern-day pilgrim hostel for those walking or cycling the Fife Pilgrim Way. There could not be a more appropriate modern use for this important medieval building.

The *hospitium* serves as a reminder of the importance of staging

Opposite
Hospitium,
Inverkeithing

posts and resting places along the pilgrim way on which people are forever moving on. Inverkeithing today is situated close to a modern staging post where travellers change direction and make connections – Ferrytoll Park & Ride off the main A90 to Edinburgh which provides important bus links across Scotland and cuts down on the number of car journeys into Edinburgh. There is another similar facility at Halbeath on the outskirts of Dunfermline. Inverkeithing Train Station also provides a bus link to Edinburgh airport. Such staging places prompt reflections about the ever-changing and transitory nature of our lives and also about the stages in our own journeys. There are times in life to stop and pause and reflect, just as there are others when it is time to move on and, indeed, to change direction. On pilgrimage, there is an emphasis on journeying and travelling, a rhythm of coming and going, of pausing and then hastening on. We depart only to return. So it is with life, and especially with the Christian life where there is both a time to pause and reflect but also a constant call to change, or *metanoia*, dying to the past and to old regrets and sins, accepting God's forgiveness and moving on to a new future. Maybe passing through or near the Ferrytoll, Halbeath Park & Ride and Inverkeithing Station, which are essentially changing places rather than destinations, can prompt and inspire thoughts about these aspects of life and faith.

Leaving Inverkeithing en route to Rosyth, the Fife Pilgrim Way crosses over the M90 motorway and the B980 and ascends Castle-landhill. This was the base of the Scottish army in the Battle of Inverkeithing, fought against Oliver Cromwell's English Parliamentary forces on 20 July 1651. The factors that led up to this battle, the bloodiest ever fought in Fife and one of the most decisive in the Civil War, paving the way for Cromwell's conquest of Scotland, are outlined in chapter 8, which discusses the complex religious and political history of Scotland in the mid seventeenth century. Suffice it to say here that Cromwell identified Fife as the key to outflanking the pro-Royalist Scottish army that was garrisoned at Stirling, and he prepared for a sea-borne assault on the coast at North Queensferry. On the night of 16 July 1651, around 2,000 men landed on the north shore of the Forth, almost certainly at Port Laing on the south side of Inverkeithing Bay. By 20 July, after further landings, the English Parliamentary force, numbering around 5,000 men in four regiments of infantry and three of cavalry, was dug in on the Ferry Hills to the south-west of Inverkeithing. The Scots forces, numbering around 4,500 in five regiments of infantry and five of cavalry and establishing their position on the slightly higher Castleland Hill to the north, were a mixed bunch made up of hardened Covenanters and Royalists, local militia from Dunfermline and Inverkeithing, Highlanders and others who had been dispatched from Stirling. On hearing a report of further Scottish reinforcements coming from Stirling, the English attacked. Despite having to advance uphill and after an initial successful Scots cavalry charge, the English gained the upper hand and the Scottish troops retreated north towards Pitreavie Castle, sustaining heavy losses as they did so. A Highland regiment under MacLean of Duart held out for four hours on the slopes around the castle despite suffering heavy losses – according to English accounts all but 35 of the 800 MacLean clansmen who fought in the battle were killed. The victory of the English Parliamentary forces was decisive and bloody. Over 2,000 Scots were killed and around 1,500 taken prisoner. The Pinkerton Burn, which runs through the valley to the west of the battle area (just to the west of the present B891 road north of Inverkeithing), was said to have run red with blood for days afterwards, while the ground next to it 'was like a harvest-field with corpses'.

A small cairn erected in 2001 by the Clan MacLean bears an inscription in Gaelic commemorating those who died. It is located next to the Busy Bees Day Nursery just off a small roundabout at the end of Castle Brae in the Pitreavie area of Dunfermline, just to the east of Pitreavie Castle and north of the A823(M) spur off the M90. A rather tired-looking and corroded interpretation board nearby gives an account of the battle. A noticeboard outside the Burgh Arms in Inverkeithing High Street also mentions it. Otherwise, despite its high number of Scottish casualties and its importance, the Battle of Inverkeithing is almost completely forgotten. The site of much of the

fighting has now been covered by roads and urban development, although the locations of the early positions, the Parliamentary camp on the Ferry Hills and the Scottish base on the slopes of Castleland Hill, are still largely undeveloped open fields. There is also an area of open land just south of the memorial cairn, soon to be built over, which is likely to have been where much of the fiercest fighting took place in the later stages of the battle. In the mid nineteenth century several skeletons were found in this area and there are likely to be many more still buried there. They provide a grim if unseen reminder of the terrible cost of war to pilgrims making their way to Rosyth, one of Britain's most important historic naval bases and recently the construction yard for the country's two biggest-ever aircraft carriers.

Opposite
Clan MacLean
cairn

# 4
# Dunfermline

Dunfermline – the name means 'the hill by the winding stream' – takes its place as second only to St Andrews in Fife, and indeed in Scotland as a whole, as a pilgrim destination. Its considerable royal connections put the crown into the symbol of the Fife Pilgrim Way and, indeed, explain why Fife is called a kingdom. The main residence of Scottish monarchs from around 1065, and a royal burgh from the 1120s, its royal status was immortalised in the opening line of the Ballad of Sir Patrick Spens, 'The king sits in Dunfermline town, drinking his blood-red wine'. The remains of the royal palace can be visited, as can the nave of the magnificent abbey, arguably the finest and most intact medieval church building in Fife. Unjustly overshadowed by its richer and more tourist-orientated neighbour, St Andrews, Dunfermline is a place of huge importance in Scotland's spiritual and cultural history and offers much of interest and inspiration to modern pilgrims.

At the heart of Dunfermline today, as it was throughout its heyday as a place of pilgrimage in the Middle Ages, is the magnificent and massive Romanesque abbey, of which only the nave now survives. It was built between 1128 and 1150 by David I on the site of the much smaller church which his parents had erected and which probably itself stood where there had been an earlier ecclesiastical building possibly associated with the Culdees (on whom see p. 101). Under David's patronage, what previously seems to have been simply a daughter house of Canterbury became a full-scale autonomous Benedictine abbey, which was further extended through the twelfth, thirteen and fourteenth centuries with the addition of a choir, transepts, lady chapel, tall lantern tower and, perhaps most important of all, the feretory chapel built onto the east end for the enshrinement of Margaret's relics in 1250. The adjoining monastery to house the growing number of Benedictine monks was also extended during this period. The first mention of the monastery buildings is in 1304, when they were burned down on the orders of the English King Edward I. The refectory and guesthouse were rebuilt in 1329.

It is clear that pilgrims came to visit and venerate St Margaret's tomb from soon after her death in 1093. A treatise written about St Cuthbert of Durham around 1160 described crowds assembling at Dunfermline to celebrate Margaret's feast day 'for there rests the holy body of the queen, whose power of sanctity the whole region of Scotland venerates and reveres'. In 1180 Margaret's tomb was moved to a position close to the high altar in the abbey and a reliquary covered with gold leaf and carved images was constructed. William the Lion is said to have experienced visions when he spent a night praying in front of it in 1199. Following the appearance of brilliant flashes of light apparently emanating from the tomb in 1245, King Alexander II and the Scottish bishops petitioned Pope Innocent IV to canonise Margaret. The Pope initially refused on the grounds that there was inadequate proof of miracles.

It may well have been to provide evidence to support the case for canonisation that a lengthy list of miracle stories was compiled. The *Miracula S. Margarite Scotorum Regine*, which appears to date from around the mid thirteenth century, lists forty-five miracles as taking place around Margaret's tomb. Most of them are healing miracles, including the curing of toothache, tumours, blindness, madness and demonic possession and the recovery of a clerk from Inverkeithing who had lost his senses through studying too hard. In many cases Margaret herself appeared and spoke to those seeking a cure, who often spent a night alone in the abbey. Several people were healed by drinking or bathing their eyes in St Margaret's fountain, which is thought to be the well still situated in the south aisle of the nave.

These miracle stories make powerful reading. Typical is one about 'a poor little woman, English by birth and race … whose arm, from the shoulder to the tip of the fingers, was so weakened by swelling of the skin and flesh that she was unable to lift it'. Having already unsuccessfully sought a cure at the shrine of St Edmund in Bury St Edmunds, Suffolk, she was visited in a dream by a lady who suggested that she visit the shrine of St Margaret. She duly went to Dunfermline, entered the abbey and while praying there 'she fell headlong to the ground before the holy altar like a lifeless stone, losing all strength in her limbs, and she lay there for about an hour, seeming to bystanders to be already close to death. But soon sadness was turned to joy, the health of her limbs restored to her' (Bartlett 2003: 75).

Whether in response to these accounts or to further entreaties from the king and bishops, Pope Innocent relented and canonised Margaret in either 1249 or 1250, granting a forty-day indulgence to anyone visiting the church on her feast day and urging 'let pious pilgrims on their sacred journey to the shrine of Christ's first chosen Apostle Saint Andrew find sanctuary and comfort at your shrine in Dunfermline'. This was the cue for a further translation of her relics, which were enshrined with much ceremony in a chapel specially built behind the high altar. The *Scotichronicon*, compiled by Walter Bower in the fifteenth century, gives this dramatic account of the enshrinement, which took place on 19 June 1250 in the presence of the eight year-old King Alexander III and his mother, Marie de Courcy:

> The king and his queen, his mother, along with the bishops and abbots and other magnates of the realm assembled at Dunfermline. There they raised the bones and earthly remains of the glorious Queen Margaret … from the stone sepulchre in which they rested for many years and with the utmost reverence raised them in a casket of firwood entwined with gold and precious stones. When the grave had been opened up by digging,

such an intense and sweet-smelling fragrance poured from it that men thought that the entire sanctuary had been sprinkled with the fragrance of spices and the scents of flowers in full bloom. And a miracle sent by God was forthcoming there. When that famous treasure had been placed in the outer church preparatory to reburial in the choir beyond the high altar, a move intended as a mark of honour, it was raised without difficulty by the holy hands of the bishops and abbots, and was being carried in procession, with instruments playing and the choir singing harmoniously. They got as far as the chancel door just opposite the body of Margaret's husband, King Malcolm (III), which lay under the arched roof on the north side of the nave, when all at once the arms of the bearers became paralysed, and because of the great weight they were no longer able to move the shrine which held the remains … At last, as they were all marvelling one to another … they heard a voice coming from one of the bystanders, but as it is believed divinely inspired, which loudly proclaimed that it was perhaps not God's will that the bones of the holy queen be translated before her husband's tomb had been opened, and his body raised and honoured in the same way. The words met with general approval, and following the advice which they conveyed, King Alexander, with companions chosen for this purpose, lifted up the casket containing the bones of the king along with that, now raised, which held the remains of the queen, without expending any effort or encountering any obstacle. They solemnly placed both coffins in tombs which had been decked out elegantly for that purpose, as the congregation sang and a choir of prelates followed in solemn procession. There God in his mercy has often worked all manner of miracles through the holy queen. (Watt 1999, vv: 297–9)

The *Scotichronicon* contains an intriguing miracle story involving a courageous knight afflicted with a terrible fever experiencing a vision in which Margaret, Malcolm III and their three sons appeared at the doorway of Dunfermline Abbey. She told him that they were hastening to Largs to defend the Scots against the Norwegian usurper, Haakon. The knight, in great pain, made his way to Dunfermline and was carried by his servants to kiss the queen's relics. As he did so, his pain and fever suddenly disappeared. At the same time, a servant came in to say that the Scots had been victorious in the Battle of Largs, which took place in 1263. This story also appears in the *Miracula S. Margarite Scotorum Regine*, suggesting that some at least of the miracles recorded in that collection must post-date the 1250 enshrinement.

Candles were kept constantly burning around Margaret's shrine. On holy days the wooden cover was raised on pulleys to reveal the shrine to pilgrims. Other relics were probably displayed in wall cupboards in the feretory chapel, among them her gospel book and her shirt or nightdress, which was removed and worn by several Scottish queens in the late stages of their pregnancies to ensure good and safe labours. There are accounts of it being taken to Mary of Gueldres before the birth of James III and to a later Queen Margaret when she was pregnant with James V. The head shrine, a gilded head-shaped case which could be opened to reveal Margaret's partially preserved skull, to which her long auburn hair was still attached, may well also have been exhibited in the abbey, possibly sometimes on the high altar.

The many pilgrims who came to Dunfermline often venerated the tombs of David I, who was widely seen as a saint, and of the national hero and liberator Robert the Bruce. A *hospitium* to accommodate them, mentioned in 1327, was dedicated to St Katherine, a fourth-century Egyptian Christian martyr who was condemned to be tied to a revolving wheel set with knives, so giving her name to the firework known as the Catherine Wheel. There were almost certainly other pilgrim hostels established in addition to the large guesthouse attached to the abbey.

From the time of Margaret and Malcolm Dunfermline Abbey became the main mausoleum for Scottish monarchs. Among those laid to rest there were Duncan II (died 1095), Edgar (1107), Alexander I (1124), David I (1153), Malcolm IV (1165), Alexander III (1285) and

Opposite
Veneration of
St Margaret's
shrine

Robert the Bruce (1329), along with many of their wives and children.

Many of these monarchs had lived in the royal palace that was established alongside the monastery. The original location of the royal residence in the time of Margaret and Malcolm Canmore is uncertain. Tradition favours the building now known as Malcolm's Tower, which stands on a rocky summit and naturally defensive site in a gorge in what is now Pittencrieff Park. All that now remains of this building is a rather unimpressive bit of wall, and recent excavations have found no evidence of construction there from before the early fourteenth century. It is possible that Malcolm and Margaret lived closer to the church which they founded on the site later occupied by Dunfermline Abbey. It is also likely that the earliest royal residence was built out of timber with a thatched roof, leaving no enduring archaeological imprint. This mode of construction probably continued for around 200 years, until the thirteenth century. The extensive monastic guesthouse seems to have been used as a royal residence from early on in its existence. The first stone-built royal palace was probably constructed during the latter part of the reign of Alexander III (1249–86), and it is from this period that the earliest surviving fragments of masonry from the palace have been dated. Edward I spent several periods living in the palace in the 1290s during his occupation of Scotland in the era of the Wars of Independence, and he planned substantial building work on it which never materialised. Instead, the palace was extensively rebuilt by his great opponent Robert I, the Bruce, in the 1320s. This was probably when it gained its final form, with four ranges grouped around a courtyard situated next to the monastery. There were further substantial alterations in Renaissance style in the early sixteenth century, especially during the reign of James V (1513–42).

The Reformation brought an end to the life of the abbey. The first Protestant cleansing of the interior seems to have taken place in September 1559 and on 28 March 1560 the altars and royal tombs were desecrated and Saint Margaret's shrine despoiled. The monks forsook the abbey and by 1563 the choir and feretory chapel were roofless and the nave, which became the Protestant parish church, was in a dangerous condition because of the state of its walls. In the 1620s the walls were shored up with buttresses, and two tiers of galleries were installed to turn the nave into a Protestant parish church focused on the preaching of the Word from a dominant pulpit. It remained in this state for the next 200 years until a new parish church was built on the site of the former choir and chancel, which had effectively become a quarry for those in search of building materials. When Daniel Defoe visited Dunfermline in 1723 he found the choir a heap of rubble, with the tombs of the Scottish kings who had been buried there lying in the open air. Today the nave stands empty, a powerful and eloquent reminder of the glory of the abbey in its medieval heyday. It is now under the care of Historic Environment Scotland and is open to the public throughout the year. The abbey's exterior is dominated by massive buttresses and exquisitely carved Romanesque doorways at the south-east corner leading from the original cloisters, and the west end. Inside, five massive pillars on the north side and six on the south support semi-circular arches with a triforium and gallery above, and a third row of arches form the clerestory. A fragment of the huge rood screen remains at the east end. The monastery also fell into disuse after the Reformation, with most of its buildings similarly being ransacked for stones. Defoe noted on his visit that the cloisters had been turned into a tennis court. Still remaining are the gatehouse known as the Pends, the massive kitchens and the refectory, with its large west window displaying the initial 'M' built into the tracery, presumably to commemorate Margaret, and part of the east range, which housed the dormitories and chapter house.

The Benedictine monks seem to have been tipped off about the Protestant assault on the abbey and managed to remove Margaret's relics. The principal relic, Margaret's head shrine, was first given to Mary, Queen of Scots in Edinburgh, then hidden in a private house and later conveyed to Antwerp in Flanders in 1597. In 1627 it passed into the hands of the Jesuits at the Scots College at Douai, a seminary founded in the north of France for the training of Scottish Roman Catholic exiles for the priesthood. It seems either to have been destroyed

or become lost there during the turbulent times of the French Revolution. The rest of the relics, together with those of Malcolm, were acquired by Philip II of Spain, and placed in two urns in the Escorial royal monastery near Madrid. A small part of the relic seems also to have come into the possession of the Scots College in Rome in 1675.

The palace was less affected by the Reformation than the abbey and went on being used by Scotland's monarchs through the later sixteenth and early seventeenth centuries. It was indeed extensively added to in the 1590s with a special residence, known as the Queen's House, being built for James VI's wife, Anne of Denmark. Three of their children were born in Dunfermline: the future King Charles I, the only British monarch and the last Scottish one to be born there; Elizabeth of Bohemia, from whom the Hanoverian line and Protestant succession of the British throne descended; and Robert, who died in infancy in 1602 and was the last member of the Scottish royal family to be buried in Dunfermline Abbey. The emigration of the royal court south to London following the union of the English and Scottish Crowns in 1603 ended the great age of the royal palace at Dunfermline, although building still went on as it did at the other Scottish palaces at Linlithgow and Holyrood. Stuart monarchs continued to visit Dunfermline – Charles II used the palace in 1650 and 1651 – but in the later seventeenth century it fell into disuse and neglect, becoming, like the abbey, effectively a quarry from which stones were taken for local building works. In 1708 the roof fell in. Queen Anne's House had become a venue for cockfighting by the mid eighteenth century, was roofless by 1789 and its site totally cleared by 1797.

What remains of the royal palace today is a long range of buildings set at the south-west edge of the monastic complex and joined to the monks' refectory by the Pends gatehouse, which Queen Anne of Denmark turned into lavish royal apartments. Showing evidence of construction and reconstruction between the thirteenth and sixteenth centuries, they comprise a kitchen, hall and lodging block, which seem to have been used by guests of the monastery as well as for the royal apartments. Like the abbey nave, the palace remains are now under

Opposite
Replica of
St Margaret's
head shrine

83

the guardianship of Historic Environment Scotland and open to the public – a combined entrance ticket secures access to both sites.

In 1821 a new parish church was built at the eastern end of the abbey, roughly on the site of the old chancel and choir, to replace the one that had occupied the nave. It is open every day from March to late October and is well worth visiting, with excellent guides on hand and much to see inside. Perhaps most immediately striking is the enormous carved pulpit of 1890, which is built over the tomb of Robert the Bruce. When the ground was being prepared for the new church in 1818, workmen came across a vault housing a skeleton encased in a lead coffin moulded to follow the contours of the body within. Below it were the decayed remains of an outer wooden coffin which had been wrapped in a linen cloth with threads of gold. Confirmation that this was, indeed, Bruce's body seemed to come from the fact that the breastbone had been severed in order to remove the heart. Bruce's dying wish was that his heart should be carried into battle against the 'Infidels' because he himself had not been able to go on a Crusade. Sir James Douglas is said to have taken Bruce's heart in a casket with him to Spain in 1330 but, in a battle against the Moors, Douglas was killed. Sir William Keith brought the heart back to Scotland and it was buried in Melrose Abbey. The skeleton was reinterred under the floor of the new church and covered in 1889 with a rectangular memorial brass embedded in a slab of marble.

Opposite
Tomb of Robert
the Bruce

It is not just the presence of this tomb and memorial that makes Dunfermline Abbey church a shrine to Robert Bruce. Its architect, William Burn, adorned the parapet of the church tower with the words 'King Robert The Bruce' in giant letters of stone. It creates a striking effect, rather like a garish modern advertising slogan, and gives Bruce a rather higher profile than Margaret in terms of visibility for those visiting the abbey today. Inside the Gothic Revival church, which is wonderfully light and airy, there are also a good many Bruce memorabilia, notably in the south transept, including a cast of his death head. There are also some particularly fine stained-glass windows. A large window at the east end, above what was probably the site of

the high altar in the medieval abbey, shows Jesus celebrating the last supper. A more recent window in the north transept designed by Gordon Webster and dedicated in 1974 as part of the commemorations of the 700th anniversary of Robert the Bruce's birth shows him alongside other Scottish nobles in the lower lights. Above them in the upper lights are Christ in Glory flanked by Ninian and Andrew on one side and Columba and Fillan on the other. It is intriguing that they were chosen over the more local boys Serf and Mungo. Although she does play rather second fiddle to Bruce, Margaret is commemorated in the south transept in a window designed by Douglas Strachan in 1932 showing scenes from her life, with the central panel depicting her marriage to Malcolm.

All that can now be seen of St Margaret's shrine is its marble base made up of fossilised seashells and brought from Frosterly near Durham, which now stands surrounded by railings in the ruins of the old feretory chapel situated outside the east end of the church. It is said that the chapel was deliberately left outside the parish church when it was built so that it could easily be accessed by Roman Catholics.

Those pilgrims wishing to venerate a relic of St Margaret today need to make their way to the Roman Catholic church at the end of East Port, a continuation of Dunfermline High Street. The supposed relic which it houses came there by a circuitous route. In 1862 Bishop James Gillis, Roman Catholic Vicar Apostolic of the Eastern District of Scotland, applied through Pope Pius IX to the Spanish royal family for the restoration of Margaret's relics to Scotland. However, despite an extensive search of the storerooms in the vast El Escorial, they could not be found. All that was eventually discovered was one small relic, thought to be a shoulder bone; this was given into the care of Ursuline nuns in St Margaret's convent in Edinburgh. The nuns later vacated the convent, which became first a Roman Catholic seminary and then archdiocesan offices and a theological library. In 2008 the relic was given to St Margaret Memorial Roman Catholic Church in Dunfermline.

This church, which is usually open from 9 a.m. to 5 p.m. on weekdays

(entrance through the small door to the left of the main doors on the south front) is well worth a visit. Built in the 1890s, it was originally designed to be as big as the abbey had been in its medieval heyday, but this ambition was never realised. A chancel, sacristy and choir vestry were added in 1936 but a proposed 174-foot circular tower at the south end of the building tapering towards the top and a substantial transept surmounted by a square tower at the crossing were never built. Inside, there is a fine canopied stone reredos behind the altar with carvings of Columba, Andrew, Margaret and Kentigern, attributed in some sources to Hew Lorimer and in others to Reginald Fairlie. A stained-glass window by Douglas Hogg depicting King David I, the largely unsung hero of the Scottish early medieval Church, was installed in 1997 together with a matching window depicting St Andrew. High up at the south end above a small gallery a brilliantly coloured rose window by John Blyth features St Margaret. Her relic is housed in the altar of the Lady Chapel to the right of the main altar. This chapel

Opposite
Panel by
Steven Foster

is also the current resting place of the replica of Margaret's head shrine, which was previously in the Abbot House Museum. Behind the altar a wooden panel painted by Steven Foster in 1986 illustrates scenes from her life, including her washing the feet of the poor. Further detailed depictions of Margaret in life and death are provided by Jurek Putter's engravings displayed in the porch area at the south end of the main church.

As at other shrines across Scotland and Protestant Europe as a whole, pilgrimages to venerate the shrine of St Margaret in Dunfermline ceased with the Reformation in 1560. They revived, however, long before the recent boom of interest in pilgrimage. The first post-Reformation pilgrimage to Dunfermline in honour of Margaret took place on 10 June 1899 and involved Roman Catholics making solemn processions to the site of the tomb and to her cave. The Catholic pilgrimage to Dunfermline was revived on a grander scale in 1930 and became an annual national event, with up to 20,000 attending. The Mass at the end of the pilgrimage was moved from St Margaret Memorial Church to the Dunfermline Athletic football ground to accommodate

the huge numbers of pilgrims. This pilgrimage ended in 1974 when the football stadium was no longer available. It was revived again in 2015 when around 1,000 pilgrims assembled in Pittencrieff Park on 28 June and walked through the town to St Margaret Memorial Church, where Mass was celebrated with ecumenical participation in the form of a Bible reading by a local Church of Scotland minister. The St Margaret pilgrimage has now become an annual event again, held in June to tie in with the anniversary of the enshrinement of her relics.

There are several other ways for modern pilgrims to Dunfermline to connect with St Margaret. One is by visiting the cave to which she is said to have resorted alone to engage in private prayer and contemplation, especially when her husband was off hunting or fighting. Originally set into the side of a steep wooded gorge, it very nearly disappeared altogether in 1962 when the town council decided to fill in the gorge to create a car park. The local outcry caused a re-think and a tunnel was built to give access to the cave from the Chalmers Street, or Glen Bridge, car park. Visitors now descend via eighty-seven steps to the sound of monastic chanting and encounter a life-size effigy of Margaret praying at the bottom. Comments on the Tripadvisor site are mixed – one likens the experience to 'descending a war-time bunker designed as a public toilet' – but generally favourable, with many pointing to the spiritual atmosphere. The cave (which another visitor misread as St Margaret's Café) is open daily between April and September and access is free of charge. It is also well worth making a visit to the superb museum adjoining the town's public library in Abbot Street, which was opened in 2017. A section on Dunfermline's royal connections includes a beautiful parian-ware statue of Margaret and she features prominently in a video display in which actors bring to life the central characters in the town's religious and royal past.

Margaret is not the only significant spiritual figure associated with Dunfermline. The town has a long association with religious as well as political radicalism and nonconformity, and especially with struggles in the mid-eighteenth-century Church of Scotland over the right of

Opposite
St Margaret's
Cave

congregations to call a minister of their choice. In 1741 Ralph Erskine, a minister in Dunfermline who had seceded from the Church of Scotland because of his unease at the influence exercised by wealthy lay patrons, known as heritors, over the appointment of ministers, built his own 'Secession Church' in Queen Anne Street. His concern, like that of many others on the Evangelical wing of the Kirk, was that heritors tended to prefer urbane, cultured, liberal 'moderate' ministers to more fervent and conservative expounders of the Gospel. Although Erskine's original church does not survive, the building that replaced it, long known as St Andrew's Erskine Church, does. It was sold by the Church of Scotland in 1998 and is now in a rather sorry state, the windows boarded up and the stonework showing signs of cracking. There are plans to turn it into a community centre. A statue of Ralph Erskine stands in front of it, a reminder of his significant role in Scotland's complex and disputatious Church history. He looks out somewhat disapprovingly over the entrance to the modern Kingsgate Shopping Centre.

Ten years after Erskine's secession, another fervently Evangelical minister, Thomas Gillespie, followed in his footsteps for similar reasons. Much involved in the religious revivals which swept through the west of Scotland in the 1740s, partly in the wake of the preaching of the English Evangelical George Whitefield, Gillespie was forced out of the Church of Scotland in 1752 for refusing to take part in the induction of a minister in Inverkeithing who had been imposed by a patron against the wishes of the congregation. He founded a new 'Relief Church', establishing its first congregation in an old meeting house in Chapel Street, Dunfermline. In the mid nineteenth century, in a rare example of Presbyterians coming together rather than splitting apart, Erskine's Secession Church and Gillespie's Relief Church joined forces to form the United Presbyterian Church of Scotland. Gillespie Memorial Church was built for this new denomination in 1849 close to the site of the Chapel Street meeting house. Located just opposite the bus station, it is now a very active Church of Scotland church, the product of further Presbyterian rapprochement with the reuniting of the United Presbyterian Church and the Free Church with the Church of Scotland in 1929. Another Church of Scotland church well worth visiting, in this case for its architectural interest, can be found at the other (southern) side of the town. St Leonard's in Brucefield Avenue was designed in 1903 by the Scoto-Catholic architect Peter MacGregor Chalmers, and features a free-standing conical-roofed tower of the kind found beside Irish monasteries and, in Scotland, at Abernethy and Brechin Cathedral.

Dunfermline's most famous son, Andrew Carnegie, was born in the upstairs room of a tiny weaver's cottage in 1835 and went on to become the richest man in the world and one of the most generous philanthropists ever. His father, William, earned 'a poor but honest' living weaving damask cloth for table linen on a hand-operated loom. His mother, Margaret, was the daughter of a shoemaker who was much involved in radical politics. Young Andrew received a solid grounding in Scottish history and folklore from his uncle, George Lauder, who delighted in telling him about heroic figures from the nation's past. He was particularly impressed by the courage and patriotism of Robert the Bruce and constantly kept in mind Bruce's famous aphorism 'if at first you don't succeed, try, try, try again', a maxim which he himself was to put into practice in a life that was an embodiment of the Victorian maxim of self-help.

The Carnegie family emigrated to the USA in 1848 and Andrew found a job as a bobbin boy in a cotton factory, where his father had also been forced to take work. Moving on to be a messenger boy in a telegraph office in Pittsburgh, he later worked as a clerk for the Pennsylvania Railroad and went on to become manager of its Pittsburgh division. Realising the enormous demand for high-quality iron and steel in the expanding railroad industry, he set up companies to make wrought-iron bridges, high-quality iron rails and later to produce steel. They made him a multi-millionaire but he was much more interested in spending money than in accumulating it. Holding that 'the man who dies rich dies disgraced', he developed his famous gospel of wealth, which expounded an approach to philanthropy not as a form of charity but as encouraging initiative and self-improvement. He endowed numerous libraries, educational institutions, community centres and concert halls. He also gave nearly 8,000 organs to churches around the world, including over 1,000 in Scotland.

Although it was a less important influence than the radical political atmosphere in which he was brought up, religion had a significant impact on the young Andrew Carnegie. His mother inherited her father's strong opposition to the harsh Calvinist tenets of Presbyterianism; his father held similar views and stopped going to church when the minister preached on the theme of infant damnation. Andrew himself eschewed any one particular denomination or creed in favour of a universalist faith which drew on the teachings of several world religions. In the words of his friend Thomas Shaw, a radical Liberal politician who also hailed from Dunfermline, 'far and wide he voyaged – to Confucius, to Zoroaster, to the world's sages – seeking the truth if haply he might find it' (Nasaw 2007: 625). Echoing the reasons that had taken his father out of conventional Christianity, Carnegie wrote in 1905 to Sir James Donaldson, Principal of St Andrews University: 'The whole scheme of Christian Salvation is diabolical as revealed by the creeds. An angry God, imagine such a creator of the universe. Angry at what he knew was coming and was himself responsible for. Then he sets himself about to beget a son, in order that the child should beg him to forgive the Sinner. This however he cannot or will not do. He must punish somebody – so the son offers himself up & our creator punishes the innocent youth ... I decline to accept Salvation from such a fiend' (Wall 1970: 219).

Andrew Carnegie reflected in later life that although as a young man he had thrown over the dogmatic theology of the Bible and Christianity, 'science brought me back to true religion'. In a draft of an inaugural address which he intended to deliver as Rector of St Andrews University in 1902 (in the event he bowed to Principal Donaldson's request that he keep off religion and instead talked about Britain's economic future), he refuted the idea that science was the enemy of religion. On the contrary, 'every discovery of science has exalted and must exalt the Creator of these startling wonders to which science alone keeps the keys'. He declared his belief 'in the truth that there is an Inscrutable Existence ... an Infinite and Eternal Energy from which all things proceed'. He went on to suggest that there was no one preferable way to refer to this 'unknown' or to worship it (Nasaw 2007: 625). Deeply sceptical of there being any existence beyond death, he wrote towards the end of his own life: 'We have this only – do our duty here, obey the judge within and bravely meet the fate awaiting us ... It is not any future I dread ... I ask for nothing better, only give us immortality here with one another ... heaven enough for me with those around me, the loved ones' (Nasaw 2007: 240).

Andrew Carnegie is an even more ubiquitous presence in Dunfermline than St Margaret. His statue stands at the entrance to the 60-acre Pittencrieff Park, which he had not been allowed to enter as a boy on the one day when it was open to the public because its owner disapproved of his family's radical politics. He bought it in 1903 and bequeathed it to his native town with the stipulation that there must be free access for everyone at all times. Declaring that 'no title is as precious in all the world as Laird of Pittencrieff', he toyed with the idea of building a house for his family in the park but decided against it. He gave $3.75 million in US steel bonds to set up a trust 'to bring into the monotonous lives of the toiling masses of Dunfermline more of sweetness and light; to give them – especially the young – some charm, some happiness, some elevating conditions of life'. This paid for the landscaping of Pittencrieff Park into what is surely one of the most beautiful, well-equipped and well-maintained public urban parks anywhere in Britain, complete with specialist gardens and glasshouses, children's play areas, concert pavilion and café. The Carnegie Dunfermline Trust also paid for medical examinations for the town's schoolchildren and set up separate medical and dental clinics for them and established Scotland's first College of Hygiene and Physical Education as well as a craft school and a Women's Institute. These were in addition to the public baths, library and gymnasium which Carnegie gave to Dunfermline. In the words of his latest biographer,

David Nasaw, 'seldom before or since has a town profited so much from the largesse of a native son' (Nasaw 2007: 643).

Carnegie's birthplace in Moodie Street is open to the public and well worth visiting. Virtually the whole of the ground floor is filled with a replica of the loom on which his father would have worked and upstairs is the small room where the family lived, ate, played and slept. Next to the tiny birthplace cottage a museum tells the story of his life and illustrates more broadly two ideals to which he was committed: philanthropy and the search for universal peace. The library which still bears his name in Abbot Street was the first of the hundreds he endowed across the world. The town's main public hall, its leisure centre and public swimming baths, the conference centre and business school attached to its further education college (Fife College) are all named after him, as is the Carnegie primary school in the aptly named Pittsburgh Road. Three grant-awarding bodies, the Carnegie UK Trust, the Carnegie Trust for the Universities of Scotland and the Carnegie Dunfermline Trust, which between them disperse large sums of money to a variety of good causes every year, are based in a new purpose-built headquarters named Andrew Carnegie House on the edge of Pittencrieff Park.

Andrew Carnegie's pilgrimage took him from rags to riches and from a narrow judgmental Christianity to a broad syncretism and universalism. To some extent, he did return to his religious roots, although perhaps not quite as firmly as Thomas Shaw suggested when he wrote in his memoirs that 'after all those voyagings, and storms of argufying, and declamatory monologue, into which an uneasiness of mind seemed ever to draw him, at last his bark landed on the Christian shore'. Carnegie's last public utterance was made at the annual dinner of the Young Men's Bible Class of Fifth Avenue Baptist Church in New York when he recalled that he had been raised in a Presbyterian nation and commented, 'That religion was a little hard for me when I was young, but I got over that' (Nasaw 2007: 625, 788). Although he did not return to Dunfermline to live, making his Scottish home at Skibo Castle near Dornoch, he never forgot his home town and was

its greatest benefactor. In many ways he seems a very different figure from the pious Queen Margaret. Yet both started out in life with the cards stacked against them, became convinced of the benefits of education and learning and devoted themselves to practical action to relieve suffering. Carnegie could have been thinking of Margaret when he observed, 'As I grow older, I pay less attention to what people say. I just watch what they do.' It is not a bad maxim for modern pilgrims to take with them as they journey on from Dunfermline.

# 5
# Fife's medieval religious communities

Monasteries, priories and friaries were a prominent feature of the religious landscape of medieval Fife. Pilgrims on the Fife Pilgrim Way can explore the ruins of three of the most important religious foundations, the Cistercian monastery at Culross, the Benedictine abbey at Dunfermline and the Augustinian priory at St Andrews. They also pass by, and may in the future be able to stay in, the guesthouse of the Franciscan friary at Inverkeithing.

It has been estimated that between the foundation of Dunfermline Abbey around 1070 and the beginning of the sixteenth century, between forty and fifty religious houses were established in Fife. They included Benedictine communities at Dunfermline, on the Isle of May (founded in 1153), and possibly also at Kilconquhar; Cistercian abbeys at Culross (1217) and Balmerino (c. 1227); and priories of Augustinian canons at St Andrews (1144), Loch Leven (1152), Inchcolm Island (1153), Abernethy and Pittenweem. Tironesian monks, so called after their mother abbey at Tiron near Chartres in France, established a community at Lindores in 1190. There were communities of Franciscan friars at Inverkeithing (1268) and St Andrews (1463); Franciscan nuns at Aberdour (1486?) and possibly also at Crail and Kilconquhar; Dominican friars at St Andrews (late thirteenth century), Cupar (1348), St Monans (1471) and possibly also at Crail, Dysart, Inverkeithing and Kinghorn; and Trinitarian friars, also known as Redfriars (an order founded at the end of the twelfth century in the area of Cerfroid north-east of Paris), at Scotlandwell (1250).

In all these religious houses men or women lived communally and intentionally under strict vows and rules, dedicating themselves to prayer, study, manual labour and evangelism. They also exercised a ministry of hospitality which involved feeding and providing accommodation for the many pilgrims who passed through Fife.

There were five distinct kinds of religious community found in Fife, as across the rest of Scotland, during the Middle Ages. The earliest in time, spanning the period from roughly the sixth to the tenth centuries, were the Celtic monks, predominantly coming from Ireland but some of whom were more local Picts or of British stock, who evangelised much of Scotland. Some of these early monks seem to have lived largely solitary lives as anchorites or hermits in imitation of the desert fathers of fourth- and fifth-century Egypt and Syria, seeking their own desert places in which to withdraw from the world and be alone with God and so giving rise to place names like Dysart. Others lived communally or cenobitically, gathering regularly through the day and night to chant the psalms in simple wooden churches and often being engaged in copying the Bible, teaching and preaching as well as in solitary contemplation. Such was the community that Serf is said to have founded at Culross, which ran a school for young boys into which Kentigern was enrolled. There also seems to have been a thriving Celtic monastic community at Kilrymont, the headland above the harbour of what would later come to be known as St Andrews.

Celtic monasticism was known for its harsh rules and severe and austere ascetic practices which included frequent bodily prostrations and genuflections, fasting and standing for long periods up to the waist in the sea or rivers. That are no surviving accounts of the life of monks in Fife from this early period but we may presume that it was similar to monastic life in other parts of Scotland and in Ireland and Wales, which is relatively well documented and about which I have written in my books *The Celtic Way* (1993), *Columba: Pilgrim and Penitent* (1997); *Colonies of Heaven* (2000); and *Following the Celtic Way* (2018).

Coming after the early Celtic monks, and possibly their direct successors in the places where they had first settled, were the Culdees. They have been the subject of much romantic embellishment and mythologising, especially among Presbyterian and Episcopalian historians, who have tended to view them as proto-Protestants displaying many of the attributes of Reformed Christianity and standing in opposition to the tenets of the Roman Church 500 years or so before the Reformation. Histories of the Scottish Church written and published in the nineteenth century portray the Culdees as having married priests, with sons often succeeding fathers, and as owing allegiance to the Abbot of Iona rather than the Pope of Rome. In fact, it is difficult to establish very much in the way of hard and fast evidence as to either the origins or the nature of the Culdee communities. There are various theories about where their name comes from – some cite the Gaelic term *Cuildeach*, meaning a sequestered person, and suggest that like the Celtic hermits, the Culdees sought to retreat from the world, while others see their origin as lying in a ninth-century reform movement within Irish monasticism known as the *Céili Dé*, or servants of God, which sought to bring a new rigour and purity to counter increasing worldliness and laxity.

There seem to have been significant Culdee communities in both Dunfermline and St Andrews before the coming of the Benedictine monks and Augustinian canons to these places. It has been postulated that the name 'Kirkcaldy' originally meant Church of the Culdees, but this is disputed by most scholars – Simon Taylor, author of *The Place Names of Fife*, says that it is a Pictish word meaning 'the hard fort'. The impression given by many Protestant Church historians, which may or may not be accurate, is that the Culdees, who also seem to have had communities on Loch Leven, at Abernethy and possibly at Culross, were more ascetic and independent-minded than those in the more regulated continental orders with whom they clashed and by whom they seem to have been suppressed and marginalised. By the end of the thirteenth century the Culdees seem largely to have disappeared from Scotland. In St Andrews in 1250 they were given

A knitted
tableau
illustrating the
life of monks at
Culross Abbey

the church and buildings of St Mary Kirkheugh, also known as St Mary on the Rock, on the headland above the harbour, perhaps significantly located outside the walls of the cathedral where the Augustinian canons held sway. This church is often taken to be the first example in Scotland of a collegiate church, served by groups of priests living a corporate life, and it is possible that such establishments here and elsewhere were a development and consolidation of Culdee communities. Overall, however, the Culdees have been shrouded in so much misty romanticism that it is difficult to make any firm assertions about them.

From the late eleventh century onwards, with the coming of monks from the new religious orders set up on the continent, many of which sought to return monasticism to the purity and simplicity of the rules first laid down by St Benedict in the sixth century, we gain a much clearer picture of the nature of life in the monasteries of Fife. They followed a regime which was less harsh and austere than that found in the earlier Irish monasteries and their Scottish offshoots, and provided a balance between prayer, meditation and devotional reading (*lectio divina*) and manual labour. Conditions were somewhat harsher for the Cistercians at Culross, who owed their origins as an order to a breakaway group of Benedictine monks who founded Citeaux Abbey in 1098. They particularly valued simplicity, with each monk being allowed only one habit, which he had to wear continuously day and night without any change of clothing. The Cistercians were also particularly wedded to self sufficiency and employed a large band of lay brothers to do agricultural work. There were strict lines of demarcation between the professed monks and the largely illiterate lay brothers, as can be seen at Culross, where there are remains of separate dormitories and refectories for the two groups.

Surviving charters and documents provide interesting insights into the everyday lives of the monks. A letter from Pope Innocent IV in 1243 acceded to a request from the Abbot of Dunfermline that 'considering the frigid region where the abbey was situated the monks might be allowed to wear caps or bonnets'. Alongside their liturgical and

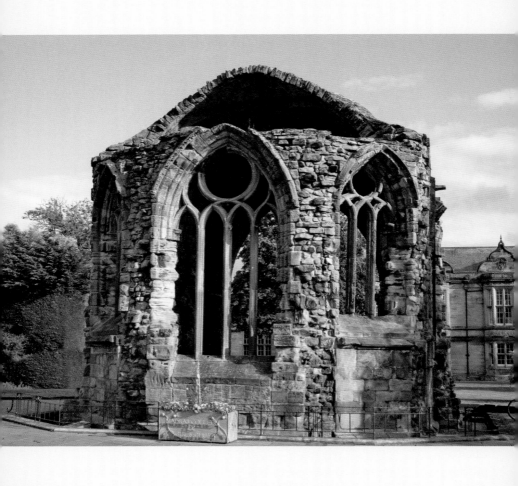

devotional duties, monks became skilled in gardening, animal husbandry, bee-keeping, brewing, book-binding, carpentry and leather and metal work. The range of their activities is well captured in a series of woollen tableaux illustrating the life of monks at Culross in the thirteenth century knitted by members of Culross Abbey Church, St Ninian's Church Craft Group, Dunfermline and the Carnegie Library Craft Group. Initially exhibited in the community gallery of the newly opened Dunfermline Carnegie Library in October 2017, they have subsequently been displayed at other venues along the Fife Pilgrim Way. The monastic ruins at Culross and Dunfermline also give some sense of the monks' lifestyle and activities, centred as they were around the communal refectory, dormitory and chapterhouse, the cloisters where the brothers would perambulate in silent contemplation and the massive abbey churches where they would regularly gather to chant the psalms and celebrate Mass. These were large communities housed in magnificent stone buildings very different from the handful of huts which accommodated the Celtic monks. The number of monks at Dunfermline Abbey appears to have increased from thirty to fifty during the thirteenth century.

Opposite
Blackfriars
Chapel,
St Andrews

The Augustinian canons who took up residence in St Andrews around 1140 lived a life similar to that of monks in many ways. Known as the black canons because of the distinctive black cloaks they wore over white tunics, they lived by the rule of St Augustine, Bishop of Hippo in North Africa in the first three decades of the fifth century. Unlike monks, regular canons were almost all ordained priests and formed clerical communities which were often attached to a cathedral, as at St Andrews, or a collegiate church. Whereas monks were largely focused on leading lives of prayer, contemplation, study and manual labour within the confines of a monastery, canons carried out liturgical, missionary, pastoral and educational duties in the community beyond the monastic walls. These included celebrating Mass, preaching, teaching and burying the dead. Augustinian canons practised a deliberately mixed life of action and contemplation, forming communities based on love, charity, mutual instruction and edification and teaching by word and example. The chapter of regular canons (so-called because they followed a rule) attached to St Andrews Cathedral, which probably numbered over seventy at its height in the mid fifteenth century, was easily the largest single religious community in Fife in the Middle Ages, and almost certainly the largest in Scotland.

Fife's fifth and last type of medieval religious community in chronological terms was made up of those in the so-called mendicant (begging) orders of the Franciscans, Dominicans and Trinitarians founded in the late twelfth and early thirteenth centuries. They represented a move away from the idea that those called to a dedicated and intentional religious life should cut themselves off from the rest of humanity and live in secluded monastic retreats. The Franciscan, Dominican and Trinitarian friars, respectively clad in their grey, black and white habits, went out into the community preaching and doing pastoral work. Committed to lives of radical poverty, they had to beg for food from those to whom they were ministering. Modern pilgrims along the Fife Pilgrim Way can gain a sense of the friars' ministry of hospitality from the imposing size and prominent position of the *hospitium* attached to the Franciscan Friary in Inverkeithing. The other main architectural relic from this branch of medieval monasticism along the route is the polygonal apse from the chapel of the Blackfriars, or Dominicans, which stands on South Street in the centre of St Andrews and serves as a reminder that for the mendicant orders, as much as those in more settled monastic communities, worship was central.

The monastic culture of the Middle Ages, based as it was on a constant commitment to conversion of life and adherence to vows of poverty, chastity, obedience and stability, seems very far away from the secular and hedonistic values of contemporary Western society. Yet there is considerable interest, sometimes in surprising quarters, in recovering some of its key principles today. Business gurus and consultants run courses based on the Rule of Benedict which they feel has much wisdom to offer in terms of good management and leadership practices. A whole new movement in contemporary Christianity promoting the formation of intentional communities goes under the name of 'the new monasticism'. Indeed, several prominent thinkers have seen the future of Christianity as lying largely with the development of monastic-style communities. The German theologian Dietrich Bonhoeffer wrote as long ago as 1935 in a letter to his brother that 'the restoration of the Church will surely come only from a new type of monasticism … I think it is time to gather people together to do this'. In his seminal work *After Virtue*, published in 1981, the Scottish moral philosopher Alistair MacIntyre drew on the example of the resilience of monasteries in the so-called Dark Ages to suggest that in 'the new dark ages which are already upon us … what matters is the construction of local forms of community within which civility and the intellectual and moral life can be sustained'. More recently, the American journalist and blogger, Rod Dreher, whose own spiritual journey has taken him from Methodism via Catholicism to the Orthodox Church, in his best-selling book *The Benedict Option* (2017) has argued that in a society which is no longer Christian, those who do still adhere to the faith should distance themselves from the world and create new communities. His particular model for these is Benedictine monasticism.

Quasi-monastic communities involving shared disciplines and a communal lifestyle have been one of the main growth areas within western Christianity over the last fifty years or so. L'Arche, a movement set up in Canada in 1968 by Jean Vanier, now has ten communities across the UK and many others abroad where able-bodied volunteers and those with profound learning difficulties live communally, committed to lives of service and worship. The Iona Community is perhaps the best-known of several dispersed religious communities whose members and associates seek to live according to a rule of life based on regular prayer, accountability and commitment to peace and justice. As the parish system breaks down, it may be that medieval-style monasticism, with its regular discipline of prayer, its collegiality and mutual support and its ministry of pastoral presence and hospitality, provides a possible model for the future of the Church. There are surely lessons to be learned in our increasingly frenzied and atomised society from the principles of balance between action and contemplation, engagement and withdrawal and solitude and community, the rhythm of prayer, meditation and manual labour and the commitment to the common life as opposed to narrow individualism which were at the heart of medieval monasticisim.

So there is much for today's pilgrims to ponder as they walk through the ruins of Fife's once mighty abbeys and monasteries. They might also ponder on the temporary, transitory and ultimately flawed nature of all human institutions, even those built for the glory of God and housing men and women trying to live out lives of radical obedience and deep faith. It was not just the Reformation of 1560 that swept away these great monuments to medieval piety and practical Christianity. Increasingly bloated and wealthy through endowments and grants of land and money, and coming to be run more and more like businesses, they had already lost much of their spiritual power, simplicity and purity by the later Middle Ages. Monarchs and others with an eye to their wealth started appointing their own relatives as lay commendators, effectively taking over authority from the abbots. In 1500 James IV installed his brother, James, Duke of Ross, as Commendator of Dunfermline Abbey. Control of the religious houses passed into the hands of royalty and the nobility.

These developments are not obvious or evident to modern pilgrims. They see rather the romantic monastic ruins and the interpretation panels describing and illustrating the activities and faith of the monks in their golden age. It is easy to romanticise and idealise medieval religious life. It had its tensions and frustrations, not least those arising from the strains of living in a tight-knit and closed community. An unnamed Abbot of Dunfermline was murdered in 1330 by one of the Cistercian monks and in 1389 Prior Robert de Montrose was murdered on the night stairs leading to the dormitory in St Andrews Priory by Thomas Plater, a canon whom he had upbraided for not following the Augustinian rule diligently enough. In many ways the dedicated religious life was a hard and demanding calling, but partly because of this it did bring men together in community and solidarity.

In both these respects, perhaps, it had similarities with another occupation which engaged many Fifers over a more recent period but which is now equally consigned to history. It was medieval monks who began mining the rich seams of coal lying under the ground and off the coast of south and west Fife. In 1291 the monastery at Dunfermline was granted a lease to exploit 'the black stanes digged from the ground', provided that they were for the monks' own use only. The remains of the collieries which were subsequently established to power the Industrial Revolution provide a constant if not always obvious feature of the landscape along the Fife Pilgrim Way from Culross through to Glenrothes and beyond. They too created tightly knit and distinctive communities which had their own deep commitment to the values of solidarity, co-operation and radical social and political action. It is time to forsake the company of the monks and start marching with the miners.

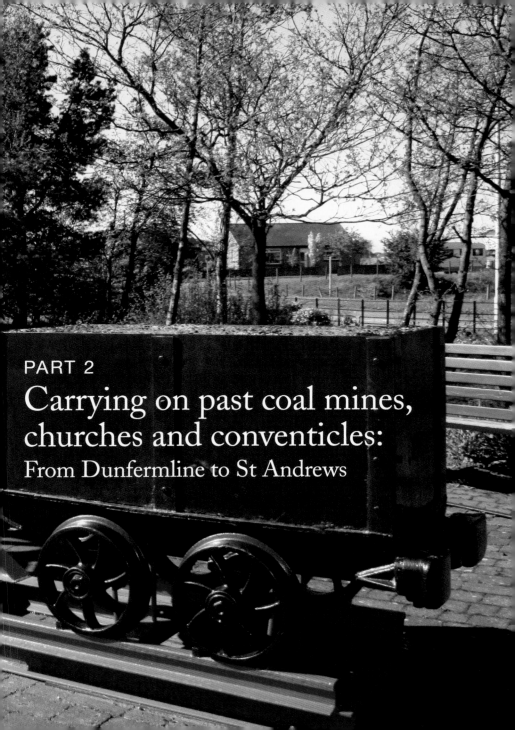

PART 2

# Carrying on past coal mines, churches and conventicles:
## From Dunfermline to St Andrews

# 6
# Marching with the miners

Although their presence is now almost impossible to detect, thanks to efforts to clean up and landscape their unsightly 'bings' or spoil heaps, former coal mines make up one of the most constant features of the landscape along the first half of the Fife Pilgrim Way. Pilgrims starting out at Culross encounter them from the very outset. The Cistercian monks there dug coal for their own use during the fourteenth and fifteenth centuries, although flooding of the mines forced them to abandon this activity several decades before the Reformation. In the early seventeenth century Sir George Bruce sank a mine shaft on the shore of the Forth and solved the problem of flooding by using a drainage system pioneered by the Ancient Egyptians and based on a continuous chain of buckets passing over a large wheel driven by three horses. Finding that there were particularly rich coal deposits beneath the waters of the Forth, he sank a further shaft on an offshore moat which he built in the bay. In 1617 James VI descended the shore shaft and after traversing the underground passage through the mines was brought to the surface via the moat shaft in the bay. Finding himself surrounded by water, his first reaction was to cry 'Treason' and he demanded to be taken back to shore by boat. In 1625 during a severe storm, high waves broke over the entrance to the offshore shaft and the underwater pit was flooded and had to be abandoned.

Those setting out along the Fife Pilgrim Way from Culross encounter the extraordinary legacy of another pioneer of underwater

Previous spread
Lindsay Colliery
memorial

mining when they skirt the northern edge of Preston Island, created in the early 1800s when Sir Robert Preston, having inherited the baronetcy of Valleyfield, reclaimed 500 acres of land from the Forth in order to sink coal mines and establish salt pans. Since 1970 huge quantities of ash slurry from Longannet Power Station have been dumped here, filling in the area between the island and the mainland. It is now possible to walk all round Preston Island and view its lagoons, which are an important haven for wildlife. This makes a pleasant and interesting 4-mile circular detour from the main Pilgrim Way, which follows the route of the Fife Coastal Path at this early stage, running through native woodland beside the old railway line which until relatively recently took coal to Longannet and Kincardine power stations.

After crossing over the railway line, the Pilgrim Way emerges onto the road from Low Valleyfield close to the site of the Valleyfield pit, established by Fife Coal Company in 1908 and finally closed in 1978. It is marked by a simple white obelisk on the shore side of the road. The Valleyfield pit was described as a 'gas tank' because of the amount of methane (also known as fire damp) it produced, which was so plentiful that it was pumped into the public gas supply. At 4 a.m. on 28 October 1939 a spark ignited the methane and coal dust in the pit and the resulting explosion killed thirty-five men, with a further twenty-six being injured. It is worth climbing up the hill to High Valleyfield to view the powerful sculpture which commemorates what was the worst ever pit disaster in Fife, and one of the worst in Scotland. It stands prominently on a grassy slope on the site of the former Miners' Welfare Club and opposite a Roman Catholic church dedicated to St Serf. A stark and graphic reminder of the terrible human cost of this industry, it depicts a mother with a baby at her breast and a young boy in shorts at her side waiting at the pit head for news. The inscription below reads:

TEARFULLY THEY CAME TO VALLEYFIELD PITHEAD
ON THAT AUTUMN DAY

Opposite
Valleyfield pit
disaster
memorial

IN PAINFUL GRIEF TO CLAIM THE DEAD
WITH DEEP RESPECT WE PRAY

Modern pilgrims continuing from Culross to Dunfermline skirt two other former coal mines, at Torryburn and Cairneyhill. Between Dunfermline and Glenrothes the Fife Pilgrim Way either goes through or passes close by a number of former mining communities, notably Wellwood, Townhill, Kingseat, Kelty, Lochore, Crosshill, Auchterderran and Kinglassie. The new town of Glenrothes was originally planned to house miners working in what was expected to be one of Scotland's most modern and productive pits at Rothes. Even those making their way along the final rural section of the Fife Pilgrim Way between Kennoway and St Andrews are treading in the footsteps of miners. There were numerous small collieries and mine workings in this part of north-east Fife between the early seventeenth and late nineteenth centuries, including significant coal mines around Ceres. They are documented in a book entitled *Mining between Ceres and St Andrews*, by local geologist John McManus published in 2010.

Perhaps the most evocative of the former mining communities which the Fife Pilgrim Way passes is the lost village of Lassoddie, which was situated just to the north of Loch Fitty four miles north-east of Dunfermline. At its height in the early 1900s, it had four working pits and a population of nearly 2,000. Following the closure of the last colliery there in 1931, the village was gradually abandoned and no trace of it remains except for the war memorial on the side of the B912 Kingseat to Kelty road shortly before it crosses the M90 motorway. It records the names of twenty-one men from there who died in the First World War. Much of this area has more recently been given over to open-cast mining, as have substantial stretches adjoining the Fife Pilgrim Way between Lochore and Kinglassie. This was, in fact, the method by which Fife's coal resources were first exploited from the sixteenth to the nineteenth centuries. With techno-logical developments and greater demand for coal in the later nineteenth century came deep mining. The Fife Coal Company was established in 1872 primarily to work the underground collieries around Kelty. It subsequently took over many other pits in West and Central Fife and became the major employer in the area.

Fife could indeed stake almost as much of a claim to be regarded as the mining kingdom as the pilgrim kingdom. So, indeed, it was described by Guthrie Hutton in his 1999 book of that title. Fife vied with Lanarkshire as the most important and productive coal-producing region of Scotland, with more than fifty pits in operation between the late nineteenth and mid twentieth centuries. The heyday of the Fife collieries came in the years leading up to the First World War, when around 20,000 miners were producing just under 10,000,000 tons of coal annually. An article in the *Dunfermline Press* of 15 September 1900 entitled 'The Fife Coalfield' confidently predicted: 'It will be a very long time ere the supply runs short. Even the quantity of "proven" coal still to work will keep the Fife miners busy for the next two hundred years, and if we add the coal in reserve, we find that the coalfield will not be exhausted until the year 2500 – six hundred years hereafter.' A Royal Commission on the prospects for Britain's coal industry reporting in 1905 was even more bullish: 'The County of Fife takes the leading position in Scotland in the matter of its coal resources. Besides the coal in this county, probably two thirds of that under the Firth of Forth will be worked by collieries in Fifeshire, so that the available resources at less than 4000 feet deep will amount to something like 5,700,000,000 tons, or sufficient to maintain the present output for 930 years.'

Fife's share of Scottish coal output rose steadily from 21 per cent in 1913 to 60 per cent in 1943. However, with falling demand for home-produced coal as Britain moved to a more oil and gas based economy, and with cheaper coal coming in from abroad, many pits closed in the 1960s and Fife's mining industry contracted drastically. The last deep mine, at Lochgannet, closed after flooding in 2002, ending underground coal mining not just in Fife but across Scotland.

The legacy left in West and Central Fife from the relatively rapid closure of so many pits was one of environmental degradation, economic decline, high unemployment and social deprivation. As has already been pointed out, the Fife Pilgrim Way has been deliberately routed through some of the former mining communities in the hope that it might bring some economic benefits, as has happened in the relatively deprived region of Galicia in north-west Spain with the development of the pilgrim way to Santiago de Compostela, with pilgrims using local shops and cafés and perhaps encouraging the development of new businesses such as guesthouses and bed and breakfast establishments. It would be good, too, if pilgrims engage with local people who were themselves miners or who carry memories of this important part of Fife's history and identity. There is much less interpretation of the coalmines than of the monasteries, and although they were more recent and more numerous figures in its landscape and history, Fife's miners have left a fainter footprint than its monks. It is important that their stories are told and their hardships, camaraderie and spiritual and political resilience are remembered. One of the differences between pilgrims and tourists is that the former do not just pass through a landscape in a coach admiring the scenery but rather interact with it, the ugly as well as the pretty parts, and let the history and experience of the people in the area through which they are passing affect them. With this in mind, it is to be hoped that those traversing the Fife Pilgrim Way will familiarise themselves with the lives and conditions in the mining communities as much as with those in the monasteries along the way.

We are fortunate to have some graphic accounts which provide moving insights into the lives of Fife mining folk at the height of the coal boom. David Rorie, who practised as a doctor in Auchterderran from 1894 to 1904, noted that when he first came there 'the great bulk of the mining population was composed of the old Fifeshire mining families, who were an industrious, intelligent, and markedly independent class. They worked in various small privately owned mines, the proprietors of which in most cases had themselves sprung from the mining class, many of them being relatives of their employees; and a certain family feeling and friendship nearly always existed.' It was only with the advent of large limited liability companies and the opening-up of more and bigger pits in the 1900s that there was a significant influx of miners from Midlothian and the west of Scotland. Rorie went on to note:

> Most of the old Fifeshire miners had dwelt for generations in the same hamlets, being born, brought up and married, and often dying in the same spot. Many of them were descendants of the old *adscripti glebae*, workers who were practically serfs, 'thirled' to pit-work for life, and sold with the pit as it changed hands. It is strange to think that this extraordinary method of controlling labour prevailed in Scotland till 1775, so that an old miner of eighty years of age at the present day might quite well be the grandson of a man who had worked as a serf in the pit. During the earlier part of the nineteenth century the different hamlets naturally kept markedly to themselves. Within living memory all merchandise required for domestic use had to be purchased at the hamlet shop, usually kept by a relation of the colliery owner; any debts incurred to him being deducted from the men's wages. To keep such a shop was therefore a very safe speculation. There were other 'off-takes', e.g. for medical attendance, pick-sharpening, etc.; and as wages were low the total sum received every fortnight on 'pay-Saturday' was often small enough. The good type of miner always handed over his wages intact to his wife, who bought his tobacco for him along with her household purchases, and returned him a sum for pocket-money, usually spent on a 'dram'. (Simpkins 1914: 386)

Although, as Rorie points out, Fife miners were no longer treated as slaves and bought and sold as commodities after 1775, conditions remained barbaric in the coal-mining industry, with children as young as eight being sent to work in the mines until well on into the nineteenth century. Before winding machinery was introduced, many women worked alongside men in the Fife pits. Traditionally, the men dug the coal and the women carried it to the surface either on their backs in baskets known as creels or by dragging trucks along steep passageways. In the early 1800s women made up one third of the workforce at Dunfermline's Baldridge colliery. An old miner told Dr Rorie about his grandmother, who was left a widow with five children, including boys of six months and two years old, when her husband was killed in a pit accident. The only way she could support her family was by herself becoming a miner: 'So she put her two boys in her coal creel, carried them down the pit and laid them at the stoop side until she digged her coals and carried them to the pit bank on her back. When she rested she gave my father a drink and my uncle a spoonful of cold stoved potatoes.' Another old miner told Rorie that the ventilation in the pits left much to be desired: 'He told me that he remembered some sixty years ago working below ground by the phosphorescent light of decaying fish-heads, in a part of the mine where the air was too foul to allow his tallow lamp to burn. He said they gave enough light to show him where to "howk" his coal' (Simpkins 1914: 387).

Rorie also noted that because of his relatively isolated situation, 'the Fifer, whether he deserves it or not, has the reputation of being more full of "freits" (superstitions) than the dweller in perhaps any other county in Scotland' (Simpkins 1914: 385). Among the many 'freits' that he observed within the mining community at Auchterderran were the beliefs that it was unlucky to start on a journey on a Friday, to turn back after you had started out from the house, or to shake hands twice on saying goodbye. To dream of the loss of fingers or teeth presaged a death and sudden silence meant that an angel was passing through the room. There were numerous instances of omens and religious customs, one such being that if two people washed their hands in a basin, the sign of the cross should be made in the water. Given the generally grim nature of life, it was perhaps not surprising that a newborn child was frequently greeted with the words, 'Ye've come into a cauld warl' noo'.

Dr Rorie's picture of an isolated and superstitious community, wary of incomers and eking out a hard and tough life with few pleasures and distractions, is largely confirmed in a detailed account entitled 'Among the Fife Miners' compiled by Kellogg Durland, an American journalist and social reformer who spent four months living and working alongside miners in Kelty in 1902. He reported that the Fife miner 'takes a great deal of knowing' and could appear dour and depressed, with one of his favourite songs being 'Like an empty ghost I go, Death the only hope I know'. However, he also discovered that 'he is a social being to be sure, the Fife miner' and provided a vivid description of one of the workingmen's clubs in Kelty, which he entered one Saturday morning at 10 a.m.:

As I slank through the doorway of a square brick building whose windows were screened to prying eyes by panes of heavy, yellow ground-glass, I instinctively pulled my hat farther over my eyes. The inner hall was piled with cases of empty bottles, and a stench of spilled liquor and dirt filled my nostrils. I paused to read a notice announcing that a collection would that day be gathered for the family of one of the members of the club who had been killed in a pit disaster. From within a room to the left came the sound of many voices above the scuffling of feet.

Suddenly the door flew wide, and two men, one of middle age, the other scarce more than a boy, clutched in each other's arms, wrestled into the hall and sprawled noisily floorwards in a half drunken tussle, pushing me into a small room: a bagatelle-board in one corner, a table wet with beer-froth and bearing a half-emptied glass of whiskey, a number of plain wooden chairs thrown about any way over a dirty wooden floor, a few flaring lithographs and tobacco advertisements tacked to a cheaply papered wall – not the cosiest or tidiest of club-rooms, surely!

I crossed to the big room opposite. About fifteen men were lolling against the bar. Here again there was a nauseating sprinkling of dirt and slopped liquor, giving the place the general appearance of a city slum public-house. At one end of the bar a glass of beer had been upset, and two men were playing dominoes exactly in the sour pool. Next to them stood two others playing draughts – playing for drinks. (Durland 1904: 145)

Although Durland saw plenty of examples of drunkenness and noted that with a population of something under 4,700 Kelty supported five public houses, three licensed grocers and one hotel, he was also impressed by the efforts to promote temperance and particularly by the Gothenburg public house, which had been established there in 1900. This was one of a number of similarly named establishments set up in Fife pit villages, including Glencraig, Crosshill, Lochore and Kinglassie, which drew on a Swedish model and sought to eliminate the profit motive in the selling of alcoholic liquor. More salubrious and well-ordered than the drinking dens like the one he had entered at Kelty, the Gothenburg public houses were run either by municipal authorities or local committees with all profits going to local improvement schemes, such as street lighting and the provision of recreation grounds and public libraries. Durland noted that some critics felt that the Gothenburg public houses actually increased drunkenness, 'clothing it in a garb of respectability and quasi-philanthropy' but he himself was inclined to feel that they diminished it: 'The liquor is freer from adulterations than in many other places; the men declare, almost unanimously, that it is much more difficult for a man who is slightly under the influence of drink to get served there than in any other place in the village; and a portion of the profits is devoted to practical purposes' (Durland 1904: 174).

The Goths, as they are still known, remain a conspicuous feature along the route of the Fife Pilgrim Way. I have counted three – the Goth Tavern on Main Street in Newmills, the No.1 Goth directly opposite the parish church on the crossroads in the middle of Kelty, and the Red Goth directly opposite the Miners' Institute in Lochleven Road, Lochore. The former Gothenburg public house in Main Street, Kinglassie, has changed its name to the Braefoot Tavern (although it is still referred to as the Goth by some of the older residents) and smartened itself up more than the other surviving Goths, which have

Opposite
Above: The Red Goth, Lochore
Below: The No. 1 Goth,

a rather forbidding and sombre appearance, at least from the outside. I wonder how many of their younger patrons associate the names of these drinking establishments more with the post-punk goth subculture known for its black clothing, pale make-up and gothic rock than with the high-minded principles which they represented in the heyday of the coal-mining industry. It is at least good that the name Goth still survives as a reminder of this important part of West Fife's cultural heritage.

Overall, Kellogg Durland was impressed by the commitment to social welfare, self-improvement and serious study displayed by the Kelty miners. He was particularly impressed by their library, which included a recreation room, a reading room and a billiard room and noted that 'the distance between the library and the nearest public house is sufficient to entirely remove temptation from any who might feel their proximity as such'. Reviewing the reading matter he found that the novels of Robert Louis Stevenson and Sir Arthur Conan Doyle were in greatest demand among the men and was also 'somewhat surprised to find that Tolstoy was read by a certain few'. He felt that:

As in most similar villages, the public house is the common social rendezvous; but in considering the social interests one must remember the friendly societies and the churches. There are three churches in Kelty. The congregations were always good, and I noticed that the proportion of men was often nearly 50 per cent. The library is much used by the men, and is doubly popular owing to the game room and the billiard room connected with it. These, of course, are excellent counter agents to the public houses, inasmuch as they supply wholesome interests. There is also a capital public baths establishment. Its chief fault is that it is small but the equipment is excellent, including a swimming tank, sprays, tubs and a steam room. Then there is a widespread interest in athletics, especially football, cricket, and cycling. In winter dancing is popular … As these interests come to take a larger and deeper place in the lives of the people, other attractions such as those afforded by the public houses and the clubs are bound to become subordinate. (Durland 1902: 376)

Durland was especially interested in the miners' religious beliefs and observances. He quoted an old Fife proverb "Ye're no' aye gaun to kirk when ye gang doon the kirkgate' and observed that 'traditionally the miner is not a pillar of the church', pointing out that it was from farming rather than mining communities that the Covenanters were largely drawn. However, he went on to say: 'My experience was that whether the Fife miner believed in the church for himself or not he was respectful of it, and when pressed argued that "the kirk was no sae bad"' (Durland 1904: 138).

According to the Scottish Church and University Almanac of 1902, Kelty's two United Free Churches (previously the Free Church and the United Presbyterian Church) claimed 433 members between them and the Established Church of Scotland 344 communicants, suggesting that around 17.7 per cent of the population of the village were attached to the main Protestant places of worship. On the first Sunday of his stay in the village Durland attended the 11.30 service in the largest church (he does not specify which it was but presumably the parish church) and declared himself 'impressed by the solidity and appropriateness of the sermon – which was delivered without notes – the heartiness of the singing (there was no organ) and the attention of the congregation. I could not see the gallery but there were about 150 people in the area, 80 of them women and girls, 20 boys and the rest men' (Durland 1904: 139).

He also attended a Sunday school picnic at 'a charming spot on a private estate' where 200 children took part in running races and generally exhausted themselves. His impressions of this event are worth quoting at some length:

At tea time the children were collected and told to sit down on the grass in a large circle and the superintendent announced that they would sing one verse of a hymn. This is what they sang:

'Lord a little band and lowly
We are come to sing to thee
Thou art great and high and holy
O, how solemn we should be.'

Poor little things – trying to be solemn at a picnic long enough
to sing their hymn. It was so very Scotch. A few moments afterwards children and teachers were up again and at play, their
fun in no way tinged with solemnity. As I sat down to take my
cookies, buns and tea, a finely formed young fellow sat down
beside me and began a conversation with the words:-

'I have only been like this a little while.'
I could not make out what he meant till he continued after
a pause: 'I was converted about a twelvemonth since.'
'Converted ? What do you mean by that?'
'Well. – By converted I mean – converted – converted –
changed from one position to another. I was in sin; now I'm
happy and peace fills my heart. I wudna change for onything.'
'Why are you? What gives you that peace?'
His answer was lovely: 'I have meat that ye know not of.'
He then told me that he worked as a brusher on the
Company's time in the Aitken pit. 'It is hard to walk a Christian
life among workmen,' he added, 'unless you walk it all the time.
They watch you so.' He and two other Christians work together
and help keep one another up. As I was interested to find out
what his beliefs were I remained reticent, and merely threw out
questions to draw him on.
'The good soul lives, the bad soul dies, or worse than dies.
It is condemned to everlasting punishment.'
'What kind of punishment ?'
'Everlasting burning and fire. We dinna ken the fuel, but it
burns.'
After that he told me about his father who for forty years has

been fond of his pipe and his whiskey and who two months ago put them all aside and now leads a Christian life. I sounded him on smoking, cards and the theatre, and he said he 'didna want ony o' them, but he wudna judge others'. (Durland 1904: 140–2)

Durland was generally impressed by the efforts of Christian groups like the Christian Endeavour Society and the YMCA in the mining villages. Although they only attracted a minority of the community, he felt that alongside the friendly societies, the libraries and the Gothenburg public houses, their influence was positive and progressive. Summing up the Church's influence on the miners, he wrote: 'I think it may be said to be real – what there is of it. "Conversion" is a scientific fact in their lives. Their religion does become a dynamic influence. It is of a homely conservative type, but as with most simple things, it is true. In a word, the religion of the Fife miner is more in his everyday life than in his prayers or his church going' (Durland 1904: 187).

Other prominent figures in Fife's mining communities later in the twentieth century were not so sure that the Church's influence was benign. The Communist miners' leaders and local councillors who became increasingly dominant in Fife politics during the 1920s and 1930s were especially critical of the Roman Catholics who had come in from Ireland and the west of Scotland to work in the pits in the years after the First World War and of the influence of their priests. The Fife miners had long had a reputation for militancy and effective industrial action – by means of a stay-down strike, they had been the first in Europe to win an eight-hour day in the 1870s – and this came to express itself in the aftermath of the First World War in a growing Communist Party which had a strong overlap with miners' unions. During the 1926 General Strike the party held regular meetings, with huge attendances. John McArthur, a Communist miners' union leader, recalled the Roman Catholic Church's reaction to the involvement of their members in it: 'I remember in Valleyfield, in West Fife, a whole lot of immigrant labourers had come in from Lanarkshire and Ireland over a number of years, and there was a very strong Catholic tendency.

There had been a colossal influx into the Party branch in Valleyfield during the miners' lock-out. This so alarmed the authorities in the Catholic Church that special priests were sent up, special campaigns conducted. And those party recruits vanished like snow off a dyke' (MacDougall 1981: 142).

The Communist cause advanced in Fife on the back of increasingly militant action by miners provoked by attempts by pit owners to cut wages and increase hours. A six-week strike in 1912 was followed by a seven-month miners' strike in 1926, when workers in other industries had gone back after just nine days of the General Strike. The economic recession of the late 1920s and early 1930s saw unemployment rising to 40 per cent among Fife miners, with those in work facing cuts to their wages. It was in this period that several Communists were elected as parish and burgh councillors. In 1928 Bruce Wallace became the first Communist member of Fife County Council. Representing Lumphinnans and Glencraig, he had been blacklisted from the pits for his leadership of the 1926 strike. In 1935 Willie Gallacher, a lifelong teetotaller and temperance campaigner who had cut his political teeth as a shop steward on Red Clydeside, was elected as Communist MP for West Fife. The first Communist MP to be elected in Britain, he held the seat until 1950, a striking testimony to the hold of Communism in Fife's mining communities which also continued regularly to elect Communist local councillors – as late as 1973 the party won twelve seats on the Lochgelly and Cowdenbeath Council. When Brigadier David Baines joined MI5 in 1974 his first task was to record members of the Communist Party in Britain. He discovered that 'nearly all of them seemed to live in Fife' (obituary, *The Times*, 30 March 2018, p. 51).

There was strong support from Fife for the anti-Franco Republican cause in the Spanish Civil War of 1936–9. This brought further tensions between Communists and Catholics, as illustrated by John McArthur's recollections of speaking at an anti-Franco rally at Bowhill:

There was a sudden growth to the meeting and continual inter-jections, insults and threats were being flung at me. Altercations broke out amongst the crowd, who were objecting to the behaviour of this section. After the meeting was over, I discovered that the section that had interrupted the meeting had come down from the Roman Catholic chapel. They had been advised to support Franco on religious grounds, to oppose the Communists, who were agents of an atheistic power. That was the first real taste of religious opposition that had expressed itself in my activities in the Fife coalfield. It was obvious that the Catholic Church was being used increasingly against the progressive movement, and this experience that I personally had in Bowhill came to be expected wherever we entered an area where there was a number of practising Catholics. (MacDougall 1981: 148–9)

Catholicism played an ambivalent role in Fife's mining communities. It was not all negative, although several of the region's most prominent left-leaning politicians came to reject it, among them Jennie Lee, who was born in Lochgelly in 1904. Her grandfather, Michael Lee, was an Irish Catholic whom she remembered believing in 'the brotherhood of man and the fatherhood of God'. Her father, James, dispensed with his father's Catholic faith and Jennie, who went on to be a towering figure in the British Labour movement in the mid twentieth century, grew up, in the words of her biographer, Patricia Hollis, 'free (give or take a temporary fascination with hell-fire) of the private guilt and public animosities of formal religion' (Hollis 1997:7).

Fife has generally experienced much less of the sectarian animosity between Protestants and Catholics found in the west of Scotland. Perhaps the Catholic–Communist antagonism provided a substitute but more likely the reason for this lack of sectarian partisanship was to be found in the working-class solidarity and strong community values fostered in mining areas. Fifers continued to be in the van of both trade unionism and radical left-wing politics throughout the latter half of twentieth century, even as coal-mining declined and ultimately collapsed in the region. Many hoped that nationalisation of the coal industry in 1947 would bring about a new dawn. It did bring concrete benefits such as the introduction of a five-day week for miners and the installation of baths at the pit heads so those coming off their shifts could wash and change their clothes before going home. However, the change of ownership did nothing to mitigate the long-term decline of coal in the face of relatively cheap oil imported from the Middle East, and most of the Fife pits were declared uneconomic and closed in the 1960s. Lawrence Daly, National Secretary of the National Union of Miners from 1968 to 1984, was a Fifer whose Catholic education had left him, he said, 'with both a considerable knowledge of Scottish poetry and a need for a strongly authoritative dogma'; he had started work at the age of fifteen as a hewer in the Glencraig colliery in 1939. He served as Communist Party agent in West Fife before forming the Fife Socialist League and eventually joining the Labour Party.

Lawrence Daly's retiral from leading the NUM coincided with the start of the national miners' strike of 1984–5, the most bitter and politically charged dispute in recent British industrial relations. Although all the West Fife underground pits had shut, the Seafield and Frances collieries near Kirkcaldy were still active, along with a number of open-cast mines, and Fife miners and their families took a leading role in the strike, marching through the streets of Lochgelly, Kirkcaldy, Cowdenbeath, Glenrothes and through Lochore Meadows, and holding open-air rallies. There were strike centres in many of the old West Fife mining villages, including Bowhill, Kennoway and Kinglassie. Fife miners were militant to the last, with more than 90 per cent of those who had gone out remaining on strike until the end of the dispute, long after resistance had crumbled in other parts of Britain. Although the legacy of the 1984–5 miners' strike was the end of British coal-mining and of militant trade unionism as it had been exercised over the previous twenty years, west Fife remained an outpost of radical left-wing politics and it was no coincidence that it provided Britain's last elected Communist councillor, Willie Clarke, who himself had started work down a pit at the age of fourteen, and who retired in

2016 after forty-three years of service, mostly spent representing the mining communities of Ballingry, Lochore, Crosshill and Glencraig on local, district, county and regional councils. The new Visitor Centre at Lochore Meadows, built in 2017, is named after him. When he opened it in April 2018 he called for a Mining Heritage Museum to be built there. I can think of no better site for a permanent exhibition dedicated to telling the story of what is rapidly becoming a forgotten part of Fife's history.

It is on the stretch of the Fife Pilgrim Way between Kelty and Kinglassie that the legacy and importance of Fife's coal-mining heritage and radical left-wing political tradition can most clearly be felt today. There are two moving memorials in Kelty. A bronze statue of a miner with his distinctive lamp and helmet, sculpted by David Annand of Kilmany, stands outside the Community Centre at the top of Main Street. It was unveiled in 1997 by Mick McGahey, the retired president of the Scottish National Union of Miners, and Gordon Brown, the local MP. The other memorial, at the end of Station Road close to its junction with the A909 from Cowdenbeath and the B996 to Kinross (rather grandly named the 'Great North Road'), stands on the site of the Lindsay Colliery, which opened in 1873 and closed in 1965. Designed by Jim Douglas and made up of a replica pit bogey, or coal wagon, and pithead wheel, it commemorates the nine men who lost their lives in an underground explosion there in 1957. It was unveiled by Mick McGahey on 14 December 1996, thirty-nine years to the day since the disaster. An annual commemoration of this terrible event, led by the clergy of the village, is held in front of the miner's statue by the Community Centre.

Walking through Lochore Meadows Country Park provides modern pilgrims with further reminders of the terrible human and environ-mental cost of the industry that was once so dominant in this area. Superficially, this is an area of great beauty and tranquillity, with wide skies, the gentle slopes of Harran and Benarty hills providing a backdrop to meadows and woodland and Loch Ore itself hosting swans, ducks and canoeists, with an extensive and much-used children's playpark

on its northern bank. It is hard to believe that the 200 acres which the Country Park now covers suffered the worst environmental degradation and pollution of all Fife's coal mining areas. Loch Ore, which had been drained in 1792 for agricultural purposes, began to be filled up from the 1900s with lagoons of sludge and black heaps of pit waste and spoil piled up in its bed. There were seven pits on the site now occupied by the meadows – the Lindsay (opened in 1873), the Nellie (1880), the Aitken (1895), Lumphinnans (1896), Glencraig (1896), the Mary (1904) and Benarty (1945). All were closed between 1954 and 1966, leaving the local unemployment rate at over 30 per cent. Many more pits occupied the wider area between Kelty and Kinglassie – Kellogg Durland counted twenty when he ascended Harran Hill in 1902.

Following the closure of the pits around Lochore, the whole area was cleared up in one of the largest land reclamation schemes ever undertaken in Britain. A replica pit-winding wheel stands at the main entrance to the Lochore Meadows Country Park (the exit for modern pilgrims travelling towards St Andrews), which opened in 1976 as 'a tribute to the people of this area who depended on coal mining for their livelihood'. The legacy of the pits is brought home in several different ways in the modern Country Park. Within the children's play area are seven named mounds representing the spoil heaps from the seven collieries in the vicinity. They are surmounted by slides, swings, tunnels, a tree house and a viewing point. This imaginative re-creation of the past, undertaken in 2010, emphasises the theme of new beginnings and indeed the Christian motif of resurrection, which could be said to underpin the whole Lochore project. There are other more poignant and stark reminders of the past. Beside the second hole of the golf course and just a few hundred yards from the Visitor Centre stands the bare and forbidding outline of the pre-cast concrete frame which supported the winding gear for the Mary Pit. Erected in 1921, it looks as though it belongs to Soviet Russia. A squat colliery railway engine in National Coal Board livery stands in front of it and the interpretative panel nearby records the names of the seventy-eight

Opposite
Miner's statue,
Kelty

miners who lost their lives in the Mary colliery between 1903 and 1965.

On a stone by the side of the road along which those walking the Fife Pilgrim Way will exit from the Country Park, just in front of a pond and diagonally opposite the Visitor Centre, a small plaque depicting a miner with his wife and two young children bears the inscription: 'Erected by the Scottish people in recognition of the struggle by Fife miners and their families during the year-long strike 1984–5'. It was unveiled in 1989 by Mick McGahey. When I visited the park in search of it, none of the four staff working in the nearby Visitor Centre named after Willie Clarke had ever heard of this plaque or knew what it commemorated. It is a sad comment on how quickly the legacy of Fife's marching miners has been forgotten.

For all its undoubted success as a leisure park, the haunt of golfers, dog walkers and water-sports enthusiasts, Lochore Meadows has rather a sad atmosphere. This is not just because of the long list of those killed in pit accidents on the interpretation board by the gaunt pithead frame. There are more *memento mori* in the inscriptions on the benches which line the shores of the loch and which have been donated in memory of loved ones. When I last walked past them, several had bunches of flesh flowers or wreaths attached to them. Perhaps more than any other part of the Fife Pilgrim Way, this is a place of sad memories and intimations of mortality, somewhere for pilgrims to reflect on the past and its tragedies.

There is a further powerful reminder of the physical scars left by mining in the two huge water-filled pits just to the north of the Fife Pilgrim Way route between Lochore and Kinglassie. These are the remains of the Westfield open-cast mine where coal extraction began in 1961 and ceased in 1986, having produced 34.5 million tons of coal and leaving what have been described as the biggest man-made holes in Europe, more than 800 feet deep. Now a hazardous eye-sore, they have been scheduled for development as an alternative or gas-fired energy park.

Equally eloquent and depressing testimony to the scars inflicted by the mining industry and its demise is provided by the forlorn and

Opposite
Mary Pit
winding gear

136

run-down state of some of the villages along this part of the route. The main Lochleven Road in Lochore is dominated by the Miners' Social Club, a massive building with a central cupola which adds a rather incongruous faded grandeur to the otherwise drab street. Although still functioning, with community activities ranging from a slimming club to martial arts, it looks in need of some tender loving care, as does the old Gothenburg Public House, now the 'Red Goth' bar, opposite. A walk through Kinglassie reveals that most of the public buildings, including the Mitchell Hall, the Community Centre, the library and the health clinic, are closed and boarded up. The Miners' Welfare Institute dominates the main street. Built in 1931 and described by John Gifford as 'a mixture of picturesque and colonial neo-Georgian, like a superior golf club', until relatively recently it housed a museum to Fife's mining heritage. However, items from the collection were pilfered and financial problems forced its closure. The miners' library has long gone. The Institute now offers bowls, pool, a bar and a function room to a diminishing number of members – its secretary says that young people somehow feel that a miner's institute is not for them and belongs to a bygone age.

Opposite
Miners' strike
memorial

It would be very sad if Fife's mining heritage did disappear from the collective memory and came to be forgotten or seen simply as an embarrassing anachronism. The miners' institutes and the Gothenburg public houses point to the values of solidarity, community, self-improvement and the public good. It would be wonderful if they could find a new lease of life as pilgrim hostels and places of refreshment. These villages desperately need investment, visitors and some cherishing and attention. Perhaps the coming of the Fife Pilgrim Way may help in some way to bring that about.

The long-neglected and largely forgotten miners who once marched to the pits and to rallies and demonstrations along the route now taken by the Fife Pilgrim Way have much to teach modern pilgrims about the bonds of community and the mutual trust and dependence born out of shared adversity. This is what Kellogg Durland concluded from his time with the Kelty miners at the beginning of the century:

Looked at from whatever point one chooses, pit work is serious labour. It has its compensations to be sure, but the amount of discomfort that pit-workers become accustomed to as part of their regular routine must be experienced to be appreciated. However severe manual labour a man may have to get his shoulder to above ground, he always has the advantage of two things which are usually lacking to the miners – a high roof above him, and daylight. The toilers in the pits must carry their own sunshine with them – and for the most part they do – and the nature of the work is such that it develops many of those qualities which go to make up splendid manliness, courage, determination, trust in their neighbours, and along with this a corresponding trustworthiness and dependence in themselves. (Durland 1904: 178)

Similar reflections come from a more recent figure associated with West Fife's mining communities, Alex Maxwell, who stood for Parliament as a Communist Party candidate and served as a 'Democratic Left' councillor on Fife Regional Council for many years until just before his death in 2013: 'Fife's mining heritage is one of boom and slump, of struggle, strikes and conflict, of relative prosperity and poverty in turn, relieved often only by an intense community spirit, which is peculiar and common to mining areas. The very nature of their work bound them together as nothing else could. Underground each depended on his neighbour to survive, and that bond remained in the communities above' (Cooney 1992: 2).

Although their suffering and hardship is nothing like as intense, dangerous or long-lasting as that of miners, pilgrims, too, especially when they are tired and blistered and soaked through after a long, hard day's walking, can experience something of this sense of mutual dependence and comradeship. Miners can teach us just as much as monks about the values and the cost of solidarity and community, looking after others and the tight bonds that are forged out of shared suffering.

Opposite
Above:
Kinglassie
Miners Welfare
Institute
Below:
Lochore Miners
Social Club

# 7
# Ancient and Modern: from Kelty to Kennoway via Glenrothes

The middle section of the Fife Pilgrim Way, between Kelty and Kennoway, is not always the most scenic. It goes through depressed former mining areas and the new town of Glenrothes. But despite their social and economic difficulties, there is a strong community spirit among the inhabitants of the villages of West Fife. There is also much of historical and spiritual interest in terms of ancient monuments and churches, including some striking modern expressions of faith in Glenrothes. On this stretch of the Pilgrim Way the very ancient stands alongside the very modern.

There is a hidden history along this part of the route which has long since been obscured by the pits and other relatively recent developments. This was the region through which Roman legions under Agricola probably travelled as they sought to subdue the Picts, notorious as fighting people and called by the Romans *Picti* or painted people, presumably because of the warpaint they wore on their faces and bodies. Lochore claims to be the place where in AD 79 Agricola established his headquarters and nearly suffered defeat. Marching north from there, the Romans refreshed themselves at the spring on the hills above Loch Leven and gave it the name *Fons Scotiae*, the well of the Scots, or Scotlandwell. A fine evocation of what the landscape in this area would have looked like in this period of Pictish and Roman conflict around AD 100 is provided in the booklet produced on the history of Auchterderran Church in 2016:

Looking all around you, you are seeing mainly trees, natural trees. Not the straight pines of the Forestry Commission but Caledonian pines with naturally curved trunks and branches and also oak, beech, birch, rowan, gorse and various shrubs with some open spaces. There are no buildings, no roads, no vehicles and no graveyards. It is without sound or noise as we know it. You would hear bird song and animal sounds. You would be able to hear the rivers running to the east, with plenty trout and maybe salmon. You may see some roe deer, hares, foxes, buzzards, crows, grouse, capercaillie, partridge, wildcats, weasels and pine martins. There would be no rabbits as they did not come to Britain until the Middle Ages. (Auchterderran Church Congregation 2016: 1–2)

Churches provide the main architectural gems in these otherwise somewhat drab townscapes. The Church of Scotland and Roman Catholic churches are for the most part still functioning as places of worship although attracting much smaller congregations than in former times. The churches of the other historic Scottish Presbyterian denominations are often largely closed, although there are thriving Baptist and Episcopal churches and several lively newer Evangelical and Pentecostal churches. In Kelty, the first settlement encountered on this stretch of the route and, with a population of 6,500, one of the largest villages in Scotland, two churches are still used for worship. St Joseph's Roman Catholic Church in Cocklaw Street is a simple but pleasing rectangular pebbledash building designed in 1922 by Reginald Fairlie, while the neo-Gothic Church of Scotland parish church was built between 1894 and 1896 in Oakfield Street, originally as a church extension from Beath to cater for the hugely increased population that resulted from the opening of new pits. There have been noticeably warm relations between these two churches for many years. In 1989, during renovation work on their building, the Church of Scotland congregation worshipped in the Roman Catholic Church. Ivor Gibson, Church of Scotland minister in Kelty from 1959 to 1965, was a strong

supporter of the miners during difficult times – it was during his ministry there that both the Aitken and Lindsay pits closed. Kelty's United Presbyterian and United Free churches have long since closed – the latter until 1974 housed the village's second Church of Scotland congregation and was more recently demolished to make way for the fine modern Community Centre, which houses a library with a very good local history section. Kelty also has an Evangelical Church occupying premises above a baker's shop in Main Street.

Lochore does not have any churches – they are to be found in the adjoining village of Ballingry, now part of a single urban sprawl which also contains Crosshill to the south. The Roman Catholic Church there, constructed in 1959 with a refreshingly plain and open wooden-beamed interior, is dedicated jointly to St Kenneth and St Bernard as the result of a union with the church in Glencraig. The Catholic primary school in Ballingry is also named after St Kenneth so there is a double commemoration here of the Irish monk who may have been an early evangelist of Fife (see p. 200). Ballingry Parish Church, which following various unions – most recently with Macainsh Church in Lochgelly in 2005 – is now dedicated to St Serf, is first mentioned in 1424 but may well have been in existence since the early fourteenth century. There is, indeed, a local tradition that it may even stand on the site of a much earlier place of Christian worship, founded by monks sent out by Serf from his monastery on Loch Leven, but this is unsubstantiated. Another intriguing but wholly fanciful piece of local folklore, which gave rise to Ballingry's nickname as 'the village of the Cross', maintains that its name derives from the Gaelic *bal*, meaning village, and the Latin initials INRI, spelling out *Jesus Nazarenus Rex Judeorum*, the inscription which Pontius Pilate decreed should be put on Christ's cross. It has also been suggested that Ballingry takes its name from the Gaelic *bal-an-righ* (the king's town) but Simon Taylor and Gilbert Márkus are fairly confident that it comes from the Gaelic *baile iongrach*, meaning oozing estate, a reference to the many springs along the slopes above the village to the west. The parish church was rebuilt in the mid seventeenth century and then remodelled on a T-plan in 1831,

Opposite
Kelty Parish
Church

with a more recent substantial extension in 1966 giving it a cruciform shape. A window in the north aisle bearing the date 1661 came originally from Inchgall Chapel close to Lochore Castle. Stained-glass windows designed by Douglas Hamilton in 1958 depict the calling of St Andrew by Christ and St Serf with Loch Leven in the background.

The first ancient monument on this stretch of the Fife Pilgrim Way is to be found just off the path between Lochore and Auchterderran. Hare Law Cairn, a Bronze Age burial mound, lies at the top of a gentle hill and offers terrific views of the Lomond Hills. Most of the stones from the cairn were removed during the eighteenth century but excavations in the 1890s revealed the foundations of a wall, beneath which were three cists (stone-built coffin-like burial chambers), two urns, kitchen utensils, teeth and bones inside a food vessel and a bronze dagger. The cairn was left open overnight to allow locals to view the discovery and the treasures were all gone by dawn. All that remains now is a mound with a tree planted to mark the site of the cairn. The hill immediately to the east of Hare Law Cairn is entirely man-made, having been built up with the spoil from the Westfield open-cast mines which was carried by conveyor belt for a distance of over a mile.

The route of the Fife Pilgrim Way continues along the B921 road towards Kinglassie, skirting the village of Auchterderran. An ancient settlement, its medieval name was Hurkendorath, which has been taken (though not by Taylor and Márkus) to mean 'the pig's head shaped hill of the oak woods' and to be a reference to the nearby ridge known locally as 'the Craigs', which was thought to be shaped like a pig's head and would have been covered in oak forests. It is worth making a very short detour to view the parish church here, which seems originally to have had strong links with St Serf's monastery on Loch Leven. The earliest reference to it is in 1059 when, according to the Registry of the Priory of St Andrews, Fothad, Bishop of St Andrews, described as 'the last one of the Celtic church', who was later to celebrate the marriage of Malcolm III and Margaret, 'granted the church of Hurkendorath to the *Keledei* of Lochleven living there devoutly and honourably in a school of virtues', along with annual dues of thirty loaves of bread, thirty cheeses and eight measures of malt.

This grant seems to confirm that the monks on St Serf's island were Culdees. There are suggestions that Queen Margaret established a pilgrim hospice at Auchterderran and, indeed, that there may have been a small Culdee community there, possibly to attend to the pilgrims passing through. Around 1144 Robert, Bishop of St Andrews, granted the island of St Serf and the church of Hurkendorath to the canons regular of St Andrews Priory. This could have been part of the wider attempt to disband the Culdees and bring their former houses under the control of the Augustinians, although it is not entirely certain that Auchterderran Church did, in fact, pass to the Priory. There is a further reference to the consecration of the church at Hurkendorath by Bishop David de Bernham in 1243. In 1250 the church is mentioned as having a Trinity friar attached to it, perhaps to minister to the pilgrims staying at the hospice.

Very little of the medieval church now remains. Auchterderran Kirk was substantially rebuilt in 1676 but demolished in 1789 when a new church was built on a T-plan on an adjoining site. In 1891 a south nave and a slender spire over the crossing were added, new lancet windows were installed, the roof was retiled and the birdcage bellcote over the west gable was given a wooden hat. Inside galleries were installed, effectively doubling the seating capacity. A chancel was added in 1931, incorporating what was possibly an original window arch from the Norman church. The church has some fine stained-glass windows, including depictions of the Good Samaritan (1905), 'Sing We to The Lord' (1912), Christ the Good Shepherd and the Risen Lord (both 1930). A relic from the seventeenth century remains in the mausoleum in the churchyard, which contains the graves of the Kinninmonth family. The date 1676 can be made out carved on the freize over its entrance doorway.

Like other medieval parishes, Auchterderran had a field known as Bowbutts where local men practised archery skills which could be called on in times of conflict. Here, the Bowbutts were next to the kirkyard. Under the instruction of the parish minister, every male aged between sixteen and sixty had to fire at least six shots from his bow at targets every Sunday after the church service. Anyone who did not turn up for this practice was fined two pence. A rather later entry in the parish records throws an interesting light on Scotland's troubled ecclesiastical history in the later seventeenth century, a topic which we will be revisiting at some length in the next chapter. In 1689 the minister of Auchterderran, Robert Glasford, was arraigned before the Privy Council for not praying for the King and Queen 'except in a disdainful manner'. He was presumably a Jacobite who was not over-enthusiastic about the ousting of James VII & II in favour of William of Orange and his wife Mary. The subsequent minister, Thomas Harvie, appears to have been dismissed for stacking sheaves of wheat on the Sabbath, but it may be that this was a cover-up for similarly unacceptable Jacobite-inclined sympathies.

Kinglassie Parish Church, which is now united with Auchterderran, appears to date back to the thirteenth century and originally to have been a simple rectangular building. After the Reformation a transept and north aisle were added to the nave. The current church building dates from 1773 and was substantially extended with the provision of a large side aisle in 1891, with galleries being installed in 1894. It is significant how many of the churches in this part of Fife were either built or extended in the 1890s, the height of the coal-mining boom, when the population of the pit villages hugely expanded. Perhaps the most unusual and moving feature inside this church is the communion table, which was installed as a memorial to those who died in the Second World War following a consultation throughout the village on how they should be remembered. The names of the nine men from Kinglassie who were killed in the war are inscribed on the side of the table.

The Kinglassie Kirk Session minutes provide some interesting glimpses into the life of the church, reminding us that the past was not a golden age free of the problems we encounter now. The minutes of 1 May 1653 record: 'diverse boys and young men did most unreverently behave themselves in both the lofts of the kirk by laughing and

Opposite
Communion
table, Kinglassie
Church

discoursing the most part of the sermon'. Two elders were deputed to sit in one of the lofts 'and take notice of these boys or young men and rebuke them'. The *New Statistical Account* of Scotland, compiled in 1836 and published in 1845, reported on Kinglassie in much more positive terms. Noting that in a population of 375, there was an average of three illegitimate births per year and three public houses, it recorded that four-fifths of the population professedly belonged to the established church which had 350 communicant members. It was the only church in the village at that time – later came a Free Church (1844) and a United Free Church (1911), both of which are now closed. Noting that the population was largely involved in agriculture, with forty farmers living in the village, as well as twenty-four weavers and a number involved in brewing and other trades, the *New Statistical Account* concluded: 'Sobriety, industry and respect for religion are qualities which, with few exceptions, mark the great mass of the population. Considerable attention is paid to neatness of dress and cleanliness of personal appearance. And in such estimation is neatness of apparel held, that the want of raiment equal in quality to that of the next door neighbour is, in some instances, viewed as a valid apology for absence from church.'

Opposite
Replica pit
wheel,
Kinglassie

Kinglassie boasts two significant medieval monuments. The older one, situated some way off the Fife Pilgrim Way route about a mile south of the village in a farmer's field, and not generally accessible to the public, is the Dogton Stone, a freestanding sandstone cross. The top portion is badly mutilated and the arms are missing. Panels on the shaft show intertwined serpents and two armed horsemen. There is also the faint outline of a cross. It is thought to date from the tenth century and it has been suggested that it may conceivably mark a victory over the Vikings by Constantine II, who ruled Scotland from 900 to 943, but this is just speculation. Much closer to the route of the Pilgrim Way, and accessed from it via a footpath which branches off to the left just behind a replica pit wheel in the garden to the rear of the Miners' Welfare Institute, is a well, described on old maps either as St Glass's well or Finglassin's Well. It may perhaps have been used by medieval pilgrims en route to St Andrews. Local volunteers have cleaned and opened it up in the hope that it will attract modern pilgrims. Its designation has led to suggestions that Kinglassie may take its name from a saint. The earliest form of its name, found in 1127, is Kilglassin – Kil is the Gaelic prefix indicating a church or religious settlement and it is often followed by a saint's name, as with Kilmartin in Argyll or Kilmacolm in Renfrewshire. The Aberdeen Breviary refers to St Glascinanus, a bishop or confessor 'who is honoured as patron at Kinglassie in Fife' and gives his feast day as 30 January. However, this is probably just a medieval attempt to explain a place name. Glaisne appears in a list of Irish saints and there is an Irish place named Kilglass. It is possible that Kinglassie is named after an Irish saint who evangelised this part of Pictland around the eighth century. However, it seems more likely that the name is derived from the Gaelic *kil glaisne* and means the church by the burn. Simon Taylor and Gilbert Márkus, who tend to favour this derivation, conclude that 'with the information available to us, it is impossible to say whether a stream gave its name to the church, which then gave rise to a fictional saint's name, or whether a real saint gave his (or her) name to the church and to the local well' (Taylor 2006: 449).

Glenrothes, which is situated almost halfway along the Fife Pilgrim Way, is the administrative capital of Fife, with the headquarters of its regional council and other public services. Its population of just under 40,000 makes it the third largest town in Fife after Dunfermline and Kirkcaldy, which both have around 50,000 inhabitants. It was one of the new towns developed in Britain in the aftermath of the Second World War and a product of the New Towns Act of 1946. The Glenrothes Development Corporation began work in 1948 with the original intention of building a town to house the many miners who were expected to work in the planned new Rothes pit. To avoid creating a single-industry community like some of the mining villages nearby, the new town plan of 1951 proposed that there should be eight non-miners for every miner. It also envisaged the town being divided into a series of 'precincts' of around 4,000–5,000 inhabitants, each with a primary school, a church and a shop. The first houses and schools were opened in 1951 and the first church (St Margaret's) in 1954. The town centre development was begun in 1955. Rothes colliery opened in 1958 but closed because of geological faults and flooding four years later. In 1959 the decision was taken to develop Glenrothes as a manufacturing centre to provide jobs and housing for overspill from Glasgow. Various electronics factories came and went and the largest private employer became the Tullis Russell paper mill in nearby Markinch; unfortunately, this went into administration in April 2015, with 374 employees being made redundant with just one day's notice.

Glenrothes suffers from having a rather soulless town centre made up of an enormous shopping precinct surrounded by car parks. There is no real focal point nor any buildings of architectural distinction. This soullessness is relieved somewhat by the playful sculptures placed on roundabouts, pavements and in other locations around the town. Many were designed by David Harding, appointed the first town artist in 1968, and Malcolm Robertson who succeeded him ten years later. The Fife Pilgrim Way avoids the town centre and is routed through the attractive Riverside Park along the banks of the River Leven, passing some rather splendid concrete hippopotami designed by Stanley Bonner in 1972, before branching north through the precincts of Pitcoudie and Balfarg.

Some welcome spiritual uplift amidst what is otherwise a very secular landscape is provided by the modern church buildings scattered around the town. The only one which modern pilgrims pass close to is Christ's Kirk in Pitcoudie, a simple square building with pyramid roof erected in 1980. Its pulpit, font, lectern and stained-glass windows come from Christ's Kirk on the Green in nearby Leslie, with which it was united in 1992. The other Glenrothes church which is well worth visiting and is often open, St Columba's, built in 1960–1, is located in the town centre close to the shopping centre and bus station. It has its own freestanding bellcote, somewhat reminiscent of a pithead frame, and does not look particularly exciting from the outside – indeed John Gifford described it as 'very boxy'. Inside it is much more interesting and impressive. The sanctuary area was designed with input from Professor James Whyte of St Andrews University to be a physical expression of Presbyterian worship. A semi-circular brick pulpit in the centre emphasises the centrality of the preaching of the word in the reformed tradition. Behind it on the north wall is a striking mural by Alberto Morrocco of the Way of the Cross. The other churches in town, most of which are generally locked, are described by Gifford in the Fife volume of the Penguin Buildings of Scotland.

Modern pilgrims passing through Glenrothes can participate in a modern version of an ancient spiritual practice, thanks to an initiative by one of the town's parish churches. St Columba's has sponsored a labyrinth which has been laid out on a grass bank in Riverside Park adjacent to the route of the Fife Pilgrim Way. Labyrinths, which have their origins in Greek mythology, have long been used by Christians as an easy and accessible form of prayer walk. One of the earliest and most famous was laid out on the floor of Chartres Cathedral in France around 1200. Its single meandering path, wandering through eleven concentric circles to reach the centre, was designed to allow those unable to visit the Holy Land to experience something of the feel and flavour of a pilgrim journey and to walk in the footsteps of Christ. Although at first sight they resemble mazes, labyrinths have no blind alleys or false trails. However twisting and winding, the path always leads to the centre and then back out again. Those walking them are encouraged to pray with their feet and bodies as well as their heads, to make a physical progress that symbolises the inner journey of faith and the return to the world to face its issues and responsibilities. The Riverside Park labyrinth was created by Peter Gardner, pioneer minister to the Visual Arts Communities of Glasgow, and is maintained by the Fife Council area services parks, streets and open spaces team.

There are other modern re-creations of very ancient spiritual symbols for pilgrims to savour as they pass through the north-eastern corner of Glenrothes. The existence of three significant prehistoric ritual sites in close proximity in this area have led to the new town being described as 'Fife's Sacred Centre'. The most striking and

Opposite
St Columba's
Church,
Glenrothes
Above:
Mural
Below:
Sanctuary

incongruous of these sites, standing right in the middle of a housing estate, is Balfarg Henge, a level platform 60 metres in diameter enclosed within a circular ditch with an earthen bank at its outer edge. Around the platform is a circle of sixteen timber posts. They mark the position of similar posts which would have originally formed an entrance to the burial area in the middle. They were later replaced by two concentric rings of standing stones, of which only two now survive. During excavations in the early 1970s, a slab-covered burial pit located close to the centre of the henge was found to contain the skeleton of a young adult with a flint knife and handled beaker. There are various theories as to how old this henge, or bank, might be – some scholars suggest that it could have been begun as early as 6,000 years ago but others date it to around 3000 BC.

Nearby, on the edge of the A92, the Pilgrim Way passes Balfarg ritual enclosure, also known as the Balfarg Riding School mortuary enclosure. This site forms part of an extensive ritual complex excavated by Historic Scotland in the mid 1980s which probably dates from early in the third millennium BC. At some later period a mound was erected over this mortuary enclosure and a ditch was cut around it. The reconstruction denotes the position of post holes found during the excavation and the earthwork of the western part of the henge is still visible.

Opposite
Above:
Labyrinth,
Riverside Park,
Glenrothes
Below:
Balfarg Henge

On the other side of the road, at the entrance to Balbirnie Park, is the reconstructed Balbirnie Stone Circle. This is a Neolithic stone circle which was later reused as a Bronze Age burial site with several cists containing cremated human remains being inserted within the boundary of the standing stones. It was excavated in 1970 and moved to its present position in 1971 in advance of widening of the A92. One of the grave slabs, with cup and ring markings, is now in the National Museum of Scotland. The eerie atmosphere here is enhanced by what look like dragons' teeth in the woods on the other side of the path – they are in fact tank traps surviving from the Second World War. It is extraordinary to think of how many people must drive down the A92 en route to Glenrothes, as I have many times over the last thirty or more years, without noticing or being aware of the significance of these prehistoric sites on either side of the road. Like Hare Law Cairn, they remind us of the importance of death, and rituals surrounding it, in the lives and faiths of our ancestors hundreds of thousands of years ago.

Intimations of mortality give way to more cheerful surrounds as pilgrims continue their way through Balbirnie Park to Markinch. This 416-acre stretch of attractive parkland and wooded gardens, with its remarkable collection of rhododendrons and exotic trees, formed the grounds of Balbirnie House, now a country house hotel but formerly the ancestral home of the Balfour family, who made their money out of coal. The Pilgrim Way emerges from the park on to Markinch Hill where there are mysterious man-made terraces which could be prehistoric defensive systems or perhaps remnants of medieval strip farming. The hill offers a superb viewpoint over the town and church of Markinch and there is a very helpful set of interpretation boards covering the history of the area and significant local worthies.

Opposite
Markinch

There have been suggestions that Markinch was once the capital of a Pictish kingdom of Fife. This thesis was advanced by the Victorian historian A.J.G. Mackay (Mackay 1896: 3) and centred around the supposed existence of a Pictish palace on Dalginch Hill, which has been identified as the mound at Northhall, about 500 metres north-east of Markinch Parish Church. Dorothy Macnab Ramsay's historical novels about Pictish kings, queens and princesses published in the 1990s, built on this idea and made much of the significance of Dalginch. The presence of a Class II Pictish stone, known as Stob Cross, on the northern outskirts of the town, close to where the Pilgrim Way enters it, could be taken as further evidence that there was an important Pictish centre here. It has a cross on one side, possibly added by Christians who may have defaced the original, and a battle scene on the other. It seems to have been defaced again in the post-Reformation period, possibly by Covenanters or by Cromwell's troops in the aftermath of the Battle of Inverkeithing.

In fact, there is no hard evidence to suggest that Markinch was a Pictish centre. The first mention of Dalginch comes in a fourteenth

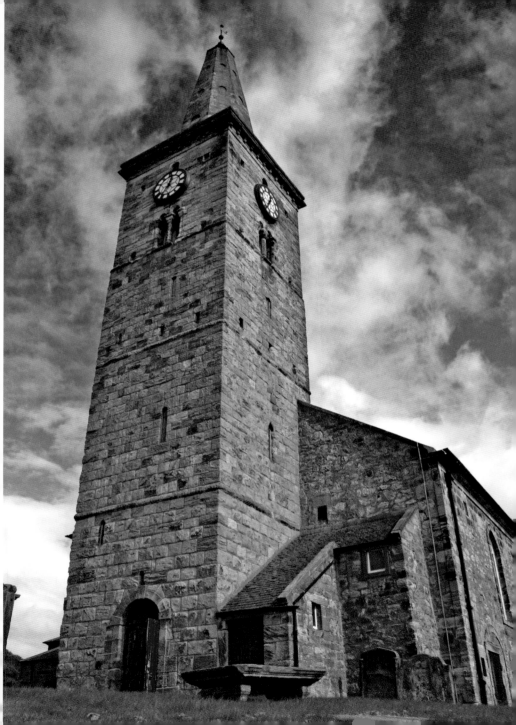

century digest of Scottish law, the *Regiam Majestatem*, which describes it as the capital place of Fife and one of northern Scotland's seven principal locations for the dispensing of justice. It seems to have been the site of a medieval moot court and it may be that the church was originally built in proximity to this important institution. Intriguingly, the church seems first to have been dedicated to St Drostan, a shadowy figure probably of Pictish descent who is largely associated with north-east Scotland. The earliest written reference to Markinch Church is a record in the Register Book of the Priory of St Andrews of around 1050, which mentions Bishop Malduin of St Andrews granting ownership of it to 'God, St Servanus and the *Keledei* of Loch Leven'. Whether Markinch went on to host a community of Culdee monks, as Auchterderran seems to have done, is unclear. The church was gifted to St Andrews Priory around 1165 and in 1243 Bishop David de Bernham rededicated it, adding St John the Baptist to Drostan to give a double dedication. A charter of 1284 granting a meadow and the right to graze two cows on it to the Augustinian canons at St Andrews makes an intriguing reference to a house nearby for the prior and canons. There has been speculation that this building may have served either as a halfway house for the use of clergy journeying between St Andrews and Dunfermline or as a pilgrim hostel. It is thought that this building, which is sometimes referred to as the Prior's House, may have stood on the site of the eighteenth-century manse, now a private house known as Mansefield, which can clearly be seen from the terrace to the east side of the church.

Opposite
Cross in nave
wall, Markinch
Church

Although nothing now remains of the eleventh-century church at Markinch, referred to in the 1050 charter entry, the Norman building which succeeded it has left a significant mark, not least in the imposing Romanesque tower which dominates the town's skyline. Bruce Manson, who has done significant research and written a detailed book on the construction of the twelfth-century church, believes that it was almost certainly built under the patronage of the MacDuff earls of Fife who lived nearby (Manson 2017). The east and west gables also date from the Norman period and chip-cut stone carving can be seen surrounding the tower as well as in reset stones on the south wall. In the early sixteenth century Prior John Hepburn undertook further building work on the church and his coat of arms can be seen on the eastern wall. The church was extended to the south in the seventeenth century and further enlargements to the north took place in 1807, when an octagonal spire was placed on top of the Norman tower, and in 1884. Recent archaeological investigations inside the church have revealed numerous masons' marks, including a distinctive cross carved on a stone at the top of the arch linking the nave with the tower. Bruce Manson suggests that 'its simplicity indicates that it was perhaps cut by a senior mason as a dedication linked to the building process rather than as as an ornamental part of the nave's overall decoration' (Manson 2017: 73). The design of this simple twelfth-century cross has been incorporated at the bottom of the logo of the Fife Pilgrim Way.

The last significant settlement on this middle stretch of the Fife Pilgrim Way is Kennoway. It stands poised between the depressed former mining communities of West Fife and the rich farming land of affluent north-east Fife. As with Kinglassie, it is not clear if its name derives from a Celtic saint, in this case our old friend Kenneth or Cainnech of Achaboe, or from a topographical description, namely the Gaelic *ceann achadh*, meaning head or headland of the field. The fact that the pre-Reformation church seems to have been dedicated to Kenneth could be taken as supporting the former derivation, although the spelling of the name as *Cenachedne* in a charter of 1148 seems to favour the latter. The 1793 *Statistical Account* offers a third possible explanation for the name, suggesting that it is derived from the Gaelic for 'the town above the cave'. There is a cave beside the burn in Kennoway Den which runs parallel to and west of the main street. Kenneth is said to have had his cell there during the period that he was evangelising this part of Fife and the cave was later supposedly used as a hiding place by the Covenanters.

Weaving and farming were for long the staple employments for the inhabitants of Kennoway. The 1793 *Statistical Account* noted that 'every person almost that is not engaged in the labours of the field is employed at the loom … All are remarkably sober, industrious, and economical … Only one instance of suicide has occurred within the last twenty years and not a person belonging to the parish has been punished for any crime or even been imprisoned, on any account whatever, during that period'. The 1845 *New Statistical Account* generally confirmed this positive verdict but did note that 'drunken brawls, and acts of wanton mischief, committed during the night by persons under the excitement of spirituous liquors, have, for a few years past, been frequent and outrageous beyond all former precedent in the history of the place'. There was a large amount of new building in the 1930s to accommodate miners from neighbouring collieries, although Kennoway never became a pit village in the sense that places like Kelty, Lochore and Kinglassie were.

There appears to have been a parish church in Kennoway from the eleventh century. Mention in a charter of 1177 suggests that, like so many other churches in mid Fife, it was given to the Priory of St Andrews. The medieval church was rebuilt in 1619. A stone with that date carved on it is built high into the east wall of the present church, which was erected in Romanesque revival style in 1850. Considerably more impressive inside than outside, it has an attractive open-beamed timber-clad roof which looks like a ship's hull and galleries with tall round-headed arcades on cast-iron columns. Colourful modern banners hang from the walls and there is a fine set of stained-glass windows by Marjorie Kemp (whose work also appears in St Leonard's Parish Church in St Andrews). Installed in 1950, they include moving images of the Good Samaritan, surely a good model for pilgrims to emulate, and of Jesus as the Good Shepherd. The pews have been removed to create a flexible worship space.

For a relatively small village, Kennoway is remarkably well supplied with places of Christian worship. The old Free Church at the southern end of its main street, where the Pilgrim Way comes in, is now an Elim Pentecostal Church and there is a small Roman Catholic Church dedicated to St Giles tucked away down a side alley. Built in 1958 and originally clad in corrugated iron, it was long known as the 'Tin

Church'. Towards the north end of the main street stands the Arnot Gospel Hall. This is worth more than a passing glance from pilgrims as they pass by on their way out of the village, as it encapsulates the extraordinary and not very edifying story of the splits, schisms and secessions that have characterised Scottish Presbyterianism. Its origins lie in the Secession Church founded by Ralph Erskine of Dunfermline (see p. 92) because of unease over ministers imposed by patrons against the wishes of congregations. Kennoway had an early group of Seceders in the 1730s who left the established kirk and initially met in fields around the town. In June 1738, Ralph Erskine preached to them on the slopes of Halfields Farm. His sermon made a deep impression on his hearers, who resolved to start a church in Kennoway. In 1750, their numbers increased when a minister was imposed on the Church of Scotland congregation, despite its opposition.

In 1751 the Kennoway Seceders were recognised as a congregation of the Associate (Burgher) Church. They built a church in 1753 – the simple but elegant sandstone building which can still be seen today – and the first minister, William Arnot, was ordained five years later. A close friend of John Newton, the slave-trading sea captain who converted to Christianity and wrote the hymn, 'Amazing Grace', Arnot apparently always preached with his eyes closed. This was said to be the result of an incident which he had witnessed while worshipping in a London church, and almost caused him to lose his composure. During the opening prayer, he heard a commotion. He opened his eyes to see a man standing on a seat and stretching up a stick with a lady's bonnet and wig on top, in an attempt to return them to their owner on the balcony above.

In 1842 the Associate Burgher Church united with the Original Secession Church (don't ask me what had originally divided them and don't get me started on the acrimonious split between the New and Auld Lichts which took place in the Kennoway congregation, as elsewhere, in the 1830s – we just won't go there) to form the United Original Secession Church. This new-found harmony lasted all of three years before another split occurred with a substantial number

Opposite
Good Samaritan window,
Kennoway
Church

of the congregation going off to join the newly formed Free Church, which had its own building in Kennoway from 1847. Those who stayed in the Secession Church linked up with members of the Relief Church to form the United Presbyterian Church in 1847. This, in turn, joined up with much of the Free Church in 1900 to form the United Free Church. In 1929 the United Free Church rejoined the Church of Scotland, precipitating a group within the congregation to form the United Free Continuing Church and worship in the Temperance Hall.

So during the nineteenth century, the Arnot Memorial Church went through at least five changes of denominational identity and spawned several breakaway groups along the way. It functioned for more than forty-five years in the twentieth century as the second Church of Scotland congregation in the village. From the early 1960s until 1974 it was led by Roy Copeland, a lay missionary, a former miner who had been seriously injured in a pit accident. Brought up as a Communist, he became a Christian through the preaching of the prominent evangelist, D.P. Thomson, who had set up a retreat centre in the village of Lassodie. In 1975 the two Church of Scotland congregations in Kennoway united, leaving the Arnot Church redundant and two years later it was taken over by a group of Evangelical Christians who had been meeting in Windygates. In 1985 they installed a large baptismal tank to allow for believers' baptism by total immersion. A Kennoway man, John Close, was the first to be baptised in this way in the Arnot Gospel Hall which now houses an autonomous Brethren Assembly, whose members meet weekly to break bread under the leadership of lay elders and without ordained clergy.

If you found all that denominational shape-shifting and factiousness rather confusing and off-putting, just wait till you get to the next stage of the Pilgrim Way and have to confront the even more complex and painful effects of similar tendencies in the seventeenth century. Be warned – there is danger ahead!

# 8
# Bloody deeds along the pilgrim way: from Kennoway to St Andrews

The final stretch of the Fife Pilgrim Way, the 22 miles or so from Kennoway to St Andrews, is easily the most rural and almost certainly the most attractive from a scenic point of view, passing through woodlands and the rich farmland of north-east Fife on a series of ancient tracks and newly laid paths. The climb up to Clatto Hill affords superb views over Largo Law and Largo Bay to the south and the Lomond Hills to the west. The banks of Clatto Reservoir provide a delightful picnic spot and the track then descends from Muirhead at the edge of fields passing the imposing ruins of Struthers Castle, which goes back to the fifteenth century, and crossing the A916 to join the Waterless Road, which has been described as the most original and significant surviving section of a major pilgrim way still to be found in Fife.

Yet, beautiful and tranquil as it undoubtedly is, there are some dark stains along this stretch of the pilgrim way. The darkest was the brutal assassination of Archbishop James Sharp on 3 May 1679. Although the murder itself took place off the route of the Fife Pilgrim Way, on what was probably the original main pilgrim and coach road into St Andrews (known also as the Bishop's Road), Sharp took broadly the same route followed by the modern pilgrim way from Kennoway to Ceres. It is said to have been over the picturesque cobbled bridge in the middle of Ceres, now known as The Bishop's Bridge and with Bishop Cottage behind it, that he clattered in his coach just a few

hours before his death. In reality, it seems unlikely that a carriage would have crossed the steep and narrow hump-backed packhorse bridge, which probably only received its episcopal name in the nineteenth century and may originally have been covered in turf rather than cobbles, when there was a ford a few yards downstream but we must not spoil a good tale. There is, in fact, enough drama in the story of Sharp's murder, whether or not he went over this bridge.

This stretch of the Pilgrim Way more than any other follows in the footsteps of the seventeenth-century Covenanters, who played an important role in the religious history of Fife and are as much silent companions along the way as monks or miners. Before plunging into the complex world of Covenanters and conventicles and outlining the background to Sharp's murder, however, we need to acknowledge some earlier bloody deeds which took place on this section of the Pilgrim Way, in the vicinity of Clatto Castle three miles or so north of Kennoway. During the late fifteenth and early sixteenth centuries the castle was the home of the Seton family, who were notorious for their violent and aggressive attacks on those passing by on what was a main highway from West Fife to Cupar and St Andrews. Their dirty deeds are graphically described in a lengthy poem of uncertain date and provenance; I have space to quote just the first four verses (the remainder can be found online at: http://www2.thesetonfamily.com:8080/history/The_Setons_of_Clatto_poem.htm):

Opposite Above: Clatto Reservoir Below: Bishop's

Laird Seton dwelt in Clato tower
Aboon deep Clato den,
He and his six freebooting sons,
Black-browed and stalwart men.

Whare'er they rode the tulzie rose,
Out-flashed the ready knife;
Until their name a byeword grew
Throughout the bounds of Fife.

At mirk the band bad sally forth
Upon their lawless way,
Prepared to plunder near and far,
To plunder and to slay.

Saint Andrews kenned them on the east,
Dunfermline on the west;
And the haill country at their hands
Was harried and oppressed.

The poem goes on to record that Laird Seton and his six sons made much use of a cave in the face of Clatto Hill which abutted the highway and also communicated directly with the castle through a tunnel. They were wont to attack passing pilgrims and travellers and drag them into the cave, where they were robbed and sometimes murdered. James IV was apparently a victim of an attack there when he was passing by on his way to hunt at Falkland. He managed to draw his sword and cut off the right hand of one of his assailants. In the subsequent confusion, the king picked up the severed hand and took it with him as he made his escape. The following day, he called in at Clatto Castle and was entertained by the laird. James asked to see his sons and while five of them were duly paraded before him, he was told that the sixth was ill in bed. The king demanded to see him and the lad eventually appeared with his arm swathed in bloody bandages. James IV produced his own bloody package and said 'Ah, you have lost a hand. I think I can fit you.' An hour later, so the poem relates, the laird and his sons were hanging dead from an ash tree beside the castle.

Nothing is now left of Clatto Castle, the earliest reference to which is in a charter dated 1550. It seems to have been sited on top of a ridge where there is now a collection of modern barns and agricultural buildings. The pilgrim way runs along the bottom of this ridge but there are no signs that I can see of any cave which might connect the ancient track and the castle. Still, like the story of Sharp's coach clattering over The Bishop's Bridge in Ceres, it is too good a tale to spoil with a cold dose of scepticism.

Before moving on to recall that other bloody deed committed along this section of the Pilgrim Way, we should pause at its midway point and pay our respects to Ceres, the only significant settlement on this part of the route and traditionally the final overnight resting place for medieval pilgrims en route to St Andrews. Set around another Bow Butts green that was once used for archery practice, it is undoubtedly one of the most attractive settlements on the entire Fife Pilgrim Way.

It has been suggested that the village's intriguing name may derive from the Roman goddess of agriculture, grain crops and fertility, Ceres, or be a corruption of a saint's name, possibly Cyriacus, a Roman nobleman put to death around AD 303 during the persecution of Christians by the Emperor Diocletian, or Cyrus, a physician in Alexandria who was tortured and martyred around the same time. In fact, it most likely comes from the Gaelic word *siar*, meaning to the west. In early documents the village is called Sireis, Seras or Syreis and Simon Taylor and Gilbert Márkus suggest in *The Place Names of Fife* that it was probably named in relation to St Andrews as 'the place to the west'. Interestingly, there were three places with biblical place names in the medieval parish of Ceres – Babylon, Sodom and Gomorrah, the last two being located on either side of a crossroads between Ceres and Pitscottie and possibly so-called because of coal-mining activity nearby. An early fourteenth-century charter pertaining to land in the parish refers to 'the public way which is called in Scots Pilgrims Gait (*Pilgrymgath*)', and also mentions a piece of land called Spitalflat, suggesting the presence of a hospital or inn for pilgrims on their way to St Andrews. It could well be that this hospice was run by a small Culdee community. In 1314 a substantial number of men from the village, under the leadership of Sir William Keith of Struthers Castle who had trained them as archers on the Bow Butts, marched to Bannockburn and took part in the famous battle in which Robert the Bruce saw off the English forces under Edward. The commemorations of this victory and of the men's safe return are said to be the origin of the Highland Games held on the Bow Butts every June, which claim to be the oldest in Scotland. A monument erected in 1914 on the bridge in the middle of the village overlooking the green commemorates 'the vindication of Scotland's Independence on the field of Bannockburn 24 June 1314 and to perpetuate the tradition of the part taken therein by the men of Ceres'.

There is much of historical and spiritual interest to engage modern-day pilgrims passing through Ceres. Among many seventeenth-century buildings is the Weigh House, which was also used as a tollbooth, gaol and courthouse. Now part of the Fife Folk Museum, which opened in 1968 and is well worth visiting, a stone tablet set over its doorway depicts a set of weighing scales with the words 'God Bless the Just' carved above them, a motto linking religious, legal and fair-trading principles. Nearby an intriguing monument on the main street depicts a Toby Jug-like character said to be the Rev. Thomas Buchanan, parish minister from 1578–99 and the last provost of the village. It was carved around 1837 by John Howie, a local stonemason who was also responsible for the panel below which shows a cavalry skirmish in the Battle of Bannockburn.

Opposite
Ceres
Above: Weigh
House scales
Below:
Buchanan effigy

The discovery in 1883 of an enamelled bronze crucifix dating from the mid twelfth century in Ceres kirkyard suggests that there may well have been a church on the site of the present parish church at that date. The earliest documentary reference to the church in Ceres comes from 1275 when it was annexed to the Collegiate Church of St Mary on the Rock, St Andrews, suggesting a possible link with the Culdee community there. The charge of Ceres Church appears thereafter to have been held in conjunction with the Provostship of St Mary's Church. Late medieval sources refer to an altar dedicated to Ninian but Taylor and Márkus are inclined to think that the medieval church was probably dedicated to the Virgin Mary. This has led my colleague George Corbett to offer yet another suggestion as to the origin of the name. He points out that in the early Middle Ages the Roman goddess Ceres' associations with fertility were transferred to the Virgin Mary and speculates that the Culdees might have chosen

the name for that reason. The present church building dates from 1806, with an impressive spire being added in 1870. It has a commanding position on a mound above the village and is well worth visiting. Its vestibule currently houses a fine effigy of a fifteenth-century Crusader knight, a reminder of another bloody and protracted conflict carried out in the name of religion. The interior of the church has a gallery and, at the time of writing, an interesting arrangement of box pews furnished with tables. For communion services these tables can be arranged into one long table at which people sit to receive the elements of bread and wine in the manner that was once common in many Scottish reformed churches and is in direct and conscious emulation of the way Jesus sat and shared with his disciples at the Last Supper. There are plans to refashion the church interior to make it more of a multi-purpose space for meetings and gatherings and this would probably mean the loss of these features. Ceres church has an open-door policy – it is always open through the day and provides a variety of aids to prayer and meditation for visitors. For modern pilgrims, it is one of the most welcoming and well-adapted of the churches along the Fife Pilgrim Way.

Opposite
Ceres Church
interior

An interpretation stone in the middle of the car park in the village centre makes much of Ceres' connection with the cult of St Andrew and the Battle of Bannockburn. Archbishop Sharp's final journey is alluded to on a notice near the car park exit and just below the sign indicating the right of way to Struthers along the Waterless Road. Slightly perversely, it points back towards the way that he had come from Kennoway rather than through the village and along the old pilgrim route to St Andrews, which became known as the Bishop's Road, via Pitscottie, Blebo Mains and St Andrews Wells towards Magus Muir, where he was to be murdered. Perhaps the good folk of Ceres are somewhat coy about being associated with this bloody deed: it may quite possibly have been in their village that he was spotted by the informant who passed the news of Sharp's presence on the pilgrim way to his would-be assassins.

To understand the reason for Sharp's murder and the brutal reprisals

which followed it, we need to plunge into the turbulent and rather murky waters of seventeenth-century Scottish religious and political history and to enter a mindset where the precise details of religious belief and affiliation were taken extremely seriously, and seen literally as a matter of life and death. We also need to recognise a tendency towards disputatiousness, legalism and intolerance that is perhaps part of the Scottish character, particularly the Scottish Presbyterian character, and a fervour bordering on fanaticism, something not absent from religion today. Mix into the pot politics intruding into religion, as it has done throughout history, nationalistic impulses, powerful egos and personality clashes, and you have a potent and not very pleasant brew.

The Scottish Reformation, which is dealt with in the third part of this book, left the country with a Presbyterian church settlement and structure different in several respects from the Anglicanism prevailing south of the border. Most notable was a strong aversion to bishops and to set liturgies and prayer books. The Stuart monarchs who ruled England and Scotland as a single united kingdom (though with separate parliaments) from 1603 onwards instinctively tended to support Anglicanism, which fitted better with their theories of divine right and monarchical authority, and to distrust the Presbyterian emphasis on the spiritual independence of the church from the state. James VI & I, who had himself been brought up in the Church of Scotland, caused considerable unease with his attempts to bring Anglican practices such as kneeling for communion and confirmation of communicants by a bishop. Several ministers who refused to go along with these practices were deprived of their living and took to holding unauthorised conventicles, defined in 1624 as 'private meetings of men and women to a private religious exercise in a time of public worship'. Often these illegal gatherings took place out of doors in remote locations, adding to the feeling that they were cocking a snook at the establishment and allowing comparison with early persecuted Christian martyrs.

James's son and successor Charles I, who came to the throne in 1625, although born in Dunfermline (where he is commemorated in a colourful plaque on the wall beneath the west end of the abbey), was even more determined to impose episcopacy and formal liturgy on his Scottish subjects. His attempts to do so in the 1630s, and specifically to introduce a Scottish Book of Common Prayer on the English model, led to a group of Scottish nobles drawing up a National Covenant in 1637 which was signed by thousands of men in churches and churchyards around the country the following year – women could swear their allegiance to the Covenant but were not allowed to sign it. Among those who signed the Covenant in Ceres was Lord Scotstarvit, previously Sir John Scot, a prominent judge and laird of the nearby Scotstarvit Tower, the remains of which still stand prominently on a hill a mile or so north of Struthers Castle and can be clearly seen by those coming down the Fife Pilgrim Way towards the A916. While vowing loyalty to the Crown, the Covenant deplored the evils and innovations introduced into the Kirk 'to the ruin of the true reformed religion' and insisted that Scotland remain Presbyterian. Charles I responded by withdrawing the proposed prayer book and allowing the General Assembly of the Church of Scotland to be called for the first time in twenty years. But the Covenanters, as the signatories of the Covenant and their supporters became known, were not satisfied and raised an army led by Alexander Leslie, Laird of Balgonie Castle near Markinch. Charles sent an army into Scotland and a brief period of conflict, known as the First Bishops' War, ensued in 1639 before terms were agreed in which the Scottish Parliament backed the General Assembly and voted that bishops had no place in it. In March 1640 a Covenanting Army marched into the north of England to support the English Parliamentary forces which were beginning to marshal against Charles under Oliver Cromwell. Scottish soldiers occupied Durham and Newcastle, forcing Charles to call the Long Parliament and to promise that Episcopacy would be abolished in Scotland. The Covenanting army returned home, although it returned south in 1644 and helped to secure the Parliamentary victory against the king at Marston Moor.

In 1643 a further document, the Solemn League and Covenant, drawn up by Alexander Henderson, Minister of Leuchars, was approved by both the Scottish Convention of Estates and the English Parliament. It sought to establish religious uniformity across the two countries on the basis of a shared Presbyterian settlement. Although the Scottish parties to the Covenant were much keener on the religious elements and the English on civil and military co-operation, the English Parliament responded by setting up the Westminster Assembly of Divines to hammer out an agreed form of Church government and doctrine for the two countries on reformed principles. This body produced the Westminster Confession of Faith, the Directory for Public Worship and a shorter and longer catechism. Although taken up in Scotland, they were never applied in England. The English Parliamentarians under Cromwell were as uneasy about imposing Presbyterianism as they were about Episcopalianism and preferred Independency, or Congregationalism, and a policy of toleration for all branches of Protestantism.

Charles I agreed to uphold the Solemn League and Covenant, as he had the earlier Covenant, and this brought many Scots to support him against Cromwell in the Civil War which now raged through the British Isles from 1642 to 1651. A Scottish army came south yet again, this time to support the Royalists against the Roundheads, and the king joined it in Newark after his defeat at Naseby in 1645. After long negotiations, he was handed over to the English Parliament in 1647 and subsequently made a prisoner at Carisbrooke Castle on the Isle of Wight. While there, he made a new alliance, known as the Engagement, with an influential group of Scottish Covenanters, henceforth known as Engagers, in which he agreed to adhere to the Solemn League and Covenant and impose Presbyterian Church government on England for a three-year term in return for military help against his English enemies. An Engager Army marched into England but was defeated by Cromwell's forces at Preston in 1648. The following year Charles I was executed, an action which brought outrage in Scotland, where there was still much loyalty to the Crown and a continuing hope that it would be the agent to make Scotland Presbyterian. Charles' son, in exile in Breda in the Netherlands, where he was persuaded to sign up to both the Covenants, was proclaimed by the Scottish Parliament as King Charles II in 1649 (he was subsequently crowned King of Scots at Scone). This was seen as a declaration of war on the part of Scotland by Oliver Cromwell, who was now presiding over England as Lord Protector. He appointed himself Commander in Chief of the Parliamentary Army and led it into Scotland. It routed the Scottish army under David Leslie at Dunbar on 3 September 1650. However, he was unable to advance further into Scotland – Leslie retreated with the bulk of the Scottish army to Stirling but kept garrisons elsewhere, notably in Fife.

Cromwell tried a twin-track approach to win over Scots from their support for the monarchy to his Republican Commonwealth and Protectorate. He sought to win the battle of the minds with more radical Presbyterians, especially those Covenanters who distrusted Charles II, and attempted to dislodge them from their Presbyterianism towards his own more radical Independency and support for lay preaching. Some Covenanters were persuaded to take a position of neutrality in the dispute between Cromwell and the king, and a few actively supported the English Parliamentarians. Others, however, like the majority of Scots, continued to be suspicious of the lay preaching, Independency and toleration for all branches of Protestantism championed by Cromwell. The Covenanters essentially remained split between Engagers, basically pro-Royalist and still looking to the monarchy as their main hope for a Presbyterian settlement, and Protestors who supported Cromwell and the Parliamentary side in the Civil War.

Cromwell's second approach was military. As already mentioned (pp. 70–73), he landed substantial forces in Fife and defeated the pro-Royalist Scottish Covenanting army at Inverkeithing in June 1651 in what was the last major battle of the Civil War in Scotland. This decisive English victory allowed him to penetrate into the heart of Scotland and crush the Covenanting opposition. By the end of July Cromwell had landed 14,000 more troops in Fife and marched on Perth, which surrendered on 2 August, cutting the Scots' line of communication to the north. It was possibly during this period that English soldiers attacked the pilgrim chapel dedicated to St James at North Queensferry (p. 50). The remainder of the Scots Covenanting army abandoned Stirling, which fell to Cromwell on 15 August, and marched into England to support Charles II. It was decisively defeated at the Battle of Worcester on 3 September 1651. The last Scots forces surrendered at the beginning of December. From then on Scotland was effectively wholly under the control of the Protectorate. Cromwell ruled Scotland with an iron grip, suppressing the Privy Council, the courts and Parliament and dissolving the General Assembly of the Church of Scotland. Eventually, in 1656, he united England and Scotland for the first time in a single Commonwealth with one Government and one Parliament. A whole variety of Protestant sects were allowed to flourish in the more tolerant atmosphere that he encouraged, including Quakers, Baptists and Independents of various kinds. This was combined with what was effectively military rule.

Among the strongholds occupied for a time by Cromwell's forces in 1653 was Struthers Castle, the ruins of which, now incorporated into farm buildings, are close to the Fife Pilgrim Way just before it crosses the A916 en route to Ceres. Two years earlier, following his coronation at Scone, Charles II had stayed there as a guest of the owner, John Lindsay. Raised to the peerage as the Earl of Lindsay by Charles I in 1633, he was a prominent Covenanting leader who had grown increasingly uneasy about the more militant and extreme Covenanters and become a strong supporter of the Royalist cause. Lindsay was not the only one to be conflicted in his Covenanting loyalties. The Church of Scotland reacted predictably to the dispute between Cromwell and Charles II by splitting into two. The Resolutioners followed the earlier Engagers in remaining loyal to the Crown and pinning their hopes on the exiled Charles II and his promise to abide by the Covenants and restore Presbyterianism to Scotland on his return as king. Their opponents, the Protestors or Remonstrants, who also styled themselves 'the Godly party' were much less sure about Charles' sincerity and intentions and felt that the Royalists were a greater threat to the Church of Scotland than Cromwell's English independents and sectaries. The two opposing factions tore the Church apart, establishing rival presbyteries and synods and not for the first or the last time weakened the witness of Scotland's national Church to the Gospel by engaging in fierce navel gazing and internecine strife.

It is at this point (readers and pilgrims alike may be relieved to hear) that we can introduce the character of James Sharp, whose progress along the old pilgrim road to St Andrews was to be so suddenly and brutally halted. Born in Banff in 1618 and educated at Kings College, Aberdeen, he entered the Church of Scotland ministry and by 1642 was employed as a regent, or junior academic, at the University of St Andrews. In 1648 he was called to be parish minister in the nearby East Neuk fishing village of Crail. Sharp increasingly involved himself in ecclesiastical politics and became a leading figure in the Resolutioner party in the Kirk, the heirs to the Engagers. He went down to London several times in the late 1650s as its representative to confer with those who wanted to overthrow the military rule of the Protectorate and restore the monarchy. Early in 1660, on the eve of Charles II's return to Britain as king, Sharp went to see him in exile at Breda to plead the cause of the Presbyterian settlement in Scotland. The two men got on well and on the restoration of the monarchy later that year, Sharp was made the king's chaplain in Scotland. In 1661 he demitted his charge at Crail to become Professor of Divinity at St Mary's College, St Andrews.

Although Sharp seems to have done what he could to get Presbyterianism established in Scotland at the Restoration, Charles II was adamant, despite his earlier subscription to the Covenants, in his determination to see Episcopalianism re-established with the restoration of the monarchy. In 1661 he announced his resolve to 'restore the church to its right government by bishops' and in May of that year episcopal government and privileges were reinstated in the Church of Scotland. Sharp accepted this royal decree and, indeed, seems to have embraced the switch from Presbyterianism to Episcopalianism with some enthusiasm. In December 1661 in Westminster Abbey he was consecrated Archbishop of St Andrews and primate of the Scottish Episcopal

Church. Many Presbyterians in Scotland felt that he had betrayed them by accepting this office and there has continued to be much debate as to whether he was motivated by personal ambition or pragmatism. Many Church of Scotland ministers followed him in becoming Episcopalians and accepting the authority of bishops, reassured by the fact that episcopacy was grafted on to the existing Presbyterian structures of kirk sessions, presbyteries and synods and that there was no attempt to impose an Anglican-style prayer book on the Kirk – in fact, there was very little to distinguish Episcopalians and Presbyterians in terms of worship throughout the seventeenth century. But others refused to accept the authority of bishops and as a result they were ousted or removed from their parishes and took to preaching at illegal conventicles, in the Covenanting tradition. Although the stronghold of these conventicles was in the south-west, there were quite a number in Fife, close to Sharp's back door.

By the mid 1660s Sharp had effectively become the King's Commissioner in Scotland and there was increasing resentment about what was taken to be his authoritarianism and high-handedness in dealing with the non-conformist ministers and their supporters. In 1668 he was the object of an assassination attempt in Edinburgh, when a Covenanter fired on him as he was getting into his coach in the High Street. This incident understandably increased his hostility towards the Covenanters and he supported the 1669 Act of Supremacy which made the king Supreme Governor over the Church in Scotland as in England, giving him unlimited power over it and consolidating his rule through bishops. Further legislation banned conventicles under pain of fines, imprisonment or corporal punishment. Sharp was active in hunting down those taking part in conventicles – in 1674 he ordered the militia to break up a conventicle at the Kinkell Braes just south of St Andrews only to be told that the members of the militia had themselves gone to hear the preacher there. Increasingly, those Presbyterians attending conventicles and refusing to worship in parish churches with 'curates' (as they were contemptuously called) who accepted episcopal authority found themselves at risk of persecution and attack from the military. The Hill of Beath near Crossgates north of Dunfermline was a prominent location for Covenanting conventicles, chosen because it provided a good vantage point from which to see the approach of soldiers. Another favoured location for conventicles on the north-east side of the Lomond Hills, also chosen because it commanded a good view of the surrounding countryside in case of attack, became known as John Knox' pulpit. Dura Den, near Kemback, and not far from Ceres, was reputedly the location of a cave to which Covenanters repaired when they were being pursued.

Rightly or wrongly, Sharp became increasingly associated with the policy of religious repression which gathered momentum through the 1670s. In July 1674 he was openly threatened on the streets of Edinburgh. By 1679 he was, in the words of his latest biographer, Julia Buckroyd, 'the single most important man in Scotland'. He was also one of the most hated, being seen by Presbyterian Covenanters as a traitor and turncoat who had through his own ambition become an agent for English Episcopalianism and arbitrary royal authority.

It is against this background that we need to read the story of Sharp's assassination on the old pilgrim road between Ceres and St Andrews on 3 May 1679. It happened when he was travelling back from a meeting of the Privy Council in Edinburgh. He broke his journey home by staying the night in Kennoway, almost certainly with his friend, Captain Seton. Local historian and Kennoway resident Dave Reid reckons that the actual house where Sharp stayed was probably slightly further up the Causeway, then the main street in the village, than the present-day Seton House, an imposing building with an intriguing Latin motto above the front door, dated 1877 and reading *Depressus ex Tollor* (Put down, I am lifted up). According to one of the more hagiographical accounts of the circumstances leading up to his murder, Sharp ate and drank very little during his overnight stay in Kennoway 'but was known to have been very fervent and longer than ordinary in his devotions; as if God, out of his great mercy, had thereby prepared him for what he was to meet with from the worst of men' (Lyon 1843, II: 93).

The archbishop set off from Kennoway on the Saturday morning initially on a track slightly south and east of the route taken by the Fife Pilgrim Way. The same rather partisan account quoted above states that throughout the journey he entertained his daughter, Isabel, who was travelling with him, 'with religious discourses, particularly of the vanity of life, the certainty of death and judgment, of the necessity of faith, good works, and repentance, and daily growth in grace'. They passed by Struthers Castle, for long the home of Lord Lindsay, who had died just a year earlier. In contrast to Sharp, and notwithstanding his own Royalist leanings, which had caused him to be imprisoned in the Tower of London and in Windsor Castle from 1651 to 1660, Lindsay had 'continued yet a zealous Presbyterian', strongly opposing the establishment of episcopacy and refusing to take the 'declaration' abjuring the Covenant. As a result of this stance, he had found it necessary in 1663 to resign all his offices and to retire from public life. He took up residence at his estate of Struthers, to 'enjoy the peace of a good conscience far from court' and died there in 1678.

There are several different accounts of the pursuit of Sharp by the nine Covenanters who were eventually responsible for his assassination. Some suggest that they had planned the deed in advance and trailed him for some time, following his coach on its journey through Ceres, Pitscottie and Blebo and along the old ridge road to Magus Muir. Other accounts suggest that the Covenanters did not originally have him in mind as a target and were rather planning to threaten and possibly beat up William Carmichael, the sheriff depute of Fife, who was responsible for much of the persecution of those attending conventicles and had established something approaching military rule over much of Fife. Learning that Carmichael was to spend Saturday, 3 May, hunting at Tarvit Hill near Ceres, twelve men had set out early that morning to look for him. However, he was warned by a shepherd about their presence and retreated to Cupar. Three of the would-be assailants had already left to go home when a boy from Baldinny reported to those remaining that Archbishop Sharp's coach had been seen passing through Ceres and heading along the coach road for St

Andrews. They deliberated about what they should do and decided that God had delivered Sharp into their hands and that their duty was to destroy him as the man ultimately responsible for imposing the hated bishops and betraying the Presbyterian cause which he had formerly championed.

Of the nine men who pursued Sharp across Magus Muir and put him to death, two were local lairds: David Hackstone of Rathillet, who nurtured a separate grievance against him, having been imprisoned when he was slow to pay the revenues of a piece of land which he farmed and which belonged to Sharp as archbishop, and John Balfour of Kinloch. Six were the sons of local tenant farmers and the ninth was a weaver from Balmerinoch (now Balmerino).

The story of the pursuit and killing has all the drama of Robert Louis Stevenson's *Kidnapped* or a John Buchan novel with rather more bloodshed. When the driver of Sharp's coach became aware that it was being followed by mounted men across the desolate stretch of moor east of the tiny settlement of Magus, he whipped up the horses and tried to make a dash for St Andrews, less than three miles away. Although initially they kept their distance, one of the pursuers eventually drew level, fired into the coach, grazing Sharp's chest, and brought the horses to a halt by slashing the postillion's face with his sword, wounding the leading horse and grabbing the reins. As the coach lurched to a halt, the other pursuers drew up, opened the door of the coach and forced Sharp out, stabbing him in the kidneys as they did so. He fell to his knees, begging for his life, only to be struck by a sword above his right eye. As he lifted up his hands in prayer, his assailants slashed at his arms and hacked at his head with such force that it is said that they split his skull, exposing his brain. All this happened in full view of his daughter and servants; the assassins rode off after removing papers, arms and valuables from the coach. According to one later account, they retired to a neighbouring cottage where they devoted themselves for several hours to prayer, thanking God for enabling them to accomplish this glorious work. One of them even claimed that he heard a voice from heaven saying, 'Well done, good and faithful servants'. Meanwhile. Sharp's shocked and numbed daughter and servants were left to load the archbishop's battered and blood-soaked body onto the coach, which then continued its slow and sad journey to St Andrews via Dewar's Mill and through the West Port. Among the many ghost stories which attach to St Andrews are several supposed sitings of a phantom coach and horses noiselessly making their way along this route.

Sharp was not buried until 17 May, a fortnight after his death. His funeral procession through the streets of St Andrews was led by sixty old men in mourning, one for every year of his life, followed by banners and standards, horses and trumpets, magistrates and members of the University of St Andrews, ministers, doctors, judges and royal officers walking in front of the highly decorated coffin. Behind it came bishops, nobles, friends and relations. A detachment of soldiers lined the route from the ruined cathedral to the door of Holy Trinity Church, where the funeral took place. The coach in which he had been riding and his bloodstained gown were paraded in the procession. Soon after the funeral, his son, Sir William Sharp, commissioned the massive monument made out of black and white marble quarried in Italy which can still be seen today in what is now called the Sharp Aisle of Holy Trinity Church. It consists of three tiers. The lowest one holds a marble relief of the murder, with the archbishop calm and serene, his raised hand symbolic of his portrayal as a saintly martyr. Flanking the relief are two Chi Rho monograms, each crowned with archiepiscopal mitres and framed by a martyr's palms. Above this lower tier, resting on three skulls, is a sarcophagus flanked by two grandiose marble pillars and two torches. On top of the sarcophagus is a full-size marble sculpture of the archbishop kneeling in prayer. An angel hands him a martyr's palm and crown. The top panel of the monument depicts what appears to be a reconstruction of the original Church of St Regulus, or St Rule, built to house St Andrew's relics. The archbishop stands beside it in full archiepiscopal garb holding his mitre. This memorial leaves one in no doubt that Sharp died as a martyr. His murder is also commemorated in the streets of St Andrews every year

Opposite
Sharp's murder
Above:
Contemporary
engraving
Below: Panel,
Sharp Memorial

in the annual Kate Kennedy procession, when a student dressed as Sharp is unceremoniously dragged out of a replica coach by fellow students clad as Covenanters.

Although extensive searches were carried out throughout Fife and Edinburgh, and substantial rewards offered for information leading to the capture of the assassins, only two were apprehended. David Hackstone of Rathillet was captured after the defeat of the Covenanters in a skirmish with Government forces at Airds Moss in East Ayrshire in 1680. He was tried in Edinburgh and condemned to death. His hands were first cut off and he was then hanged, his body dismembered and exhibited in various locations around the country. A similar fate befell Andrew Guillan, the weaver from Balmerino, who was arrested in 1683 and executed in Edinburgh. His head was stuck on a pole and exhibited in Cupar and his body hung in chains on Magus Muir. One account states that friends took down his body and buried it on the spot. There is said to have been a monument to him on Magus Muir but there is no sign of it now. There is, however, a memorial stone to Guillan still standing among trees just to the west of Claremont Farm half a mile south of Magus Muir. Erected in the early eighteenth century and restored in 1877, it has an inscription which begins:

> A faithful martyr here doth lie,
> A witness against perjury.
> Who cruelly was put to death,
> To gratify proud prelate's wrath.

William Dingwall, one of the tenant farmers involved in the assassination, was shot dead at the battle of Drumclog in South Ayrshire in June 1679 in which 200 armed Covenanters routed Government troops under the command of John Graham of Claverhouse. The remaining six assassins were never caught. John Balfour of Kinloch, described in the *Biographia Scoticana*, a book about sixteenth- and seventeenth-century Scots worthies published in 1782, as 'the principal actor in killing that arch-traitor to the Lord and his Christ, James Sharp', was tried in his absence and declared a fugitive and outlaw, but despite a reward of 10,000 marks being offered for information leading to his capture, he remained free and went on to command Covenanting forces at Drumclog and the Battle of Bothwell Brig (also in June 1679), in which a Government force of 5,000 under the Duke of Montrose decisively defeated a Covenanting army of over 4,000. Balfour later escaped to Holland, where he joined Prince William of Orange.

Several Covenanters who had no involvement at all in Sharp's murder were killed in the reprisals taken in its aftermath. On the day of the murder itself a young local man, Andrew Aytoun of Inchdairnie, was shot by Captain Dobie, a local militia leader acting on orders of the sheriff depute, William Carmichael. He was interrogated about the murder, about which he refused to say anything, and subsequently died of his wounds. Five Covenanters, who were captured at the Battle of Bothwell Brig and refused to sign a bond not to rebel again, were hanged in chains on Magus Muir on 25 November 1679 near the site of Sharp's murder. Their grave lies in what is now a ploughed field. Restored in 1877, it can be visited today.

In the woodland nearby, a stone pyramid erected in 1877 and surrounded by yew trees marks the presumed place of Sharp's murder. Eight different accounts of the event appeared within four years – four were pro-Covenanter, essentially justifying the deed and portraying Sharp as a traitor to Presbyterianism and an ambitious and venal rogue, three were pro-Sharp, portraying him as a pious and compassionate martyr and his attackers as bigoted fanatics, and one was written by an anonymous moderate Presbyterian, equally opposed to the episcopal establishment of the Scottish Church and to the murder itself, who sought to play down the importance of the act and to suggest it was essentially carried out by those who had a personal grievance against Sharp.

How should we view this controversial churchman, perhaps at once the most hated and ill-fated man to travel the Fife Pilgrim Way? He was a politician as much as a spiritual leader (he would not be the first or the last bishop of whom that could be said), a pragmatist who probably tried his best to achieve a Presbyterian Church settlement for Scotland. His fervent support for the Resolutioner party in the Kirk and opposition to the Protestors was perhaps the decisive defining issue of his life. When he realised the total immobility and implacability of the king, he was happy to throw in his lot with Episcopalianism, to take the Archbishopric offered to him and indeed to become a fierce persecutor of the more die-hard adherents to the Presbyterianism in which he had grown up and of which he had once been a champion. His biographer, Julia Buckroyd, describes him as 'the last in the long line of Scottish medieval "political" bishops which included Cardinal Beaton and Archbishop Spottiswood'. She sees him above all as a conservative: 'like many another in seventeenth-century Scotland he was alarmed by the revolutionary implications of the attitudes of some among the ministers. He was a supporter of kings and nobles and of the long-established social order' (Buckroyd 1987: 118). It was this conservatism that made him condone the use of military force against his own countrymen and former co-religionists. He should perhaps be remembered as a pragmatist who, like the English philosopher Thomas Hobbes, who died in the same year, above all sought stability and order in what were extremely violent and troubled times – not quite the martyr that he is still seen as in some Episcopalian circles, nor yet the turncoat and traitor deserving all that he got which is how he continues to be regarded by some Presbyterians.

And what of the Covenanters who pursued him along the pilgrim way and murdered him? Should they too, at least the ones who were themselves put to death, be regarded as martyrs and men of God, following their consciences and what they took to be the teaching of the Bible, or were they religious bigots and fanatics, not totally dissimilar from the Taliban terrorists or adherents of Daesh or the so-called Islamic State today? Sharp's death directly ushered in that terrible period of Scottish history known as 'The Killing Times' which lasted through the 1680s, during which those attending conventicles were savagely hunted down and persecuted, and many Covenanters were put to death. They included several Fifers, among them three weavers from Kinneuchar who were hanged in Edinburgh in 1681, their severed heads subsequently being stuck on spikes and displayed to deter others of a like mind. There is no doubt that the Covenanters did suffer appallingly for their beliefs but there is no doubt also that they showed a rigidity of view bordering on fanaticism, and the appalling savagery which Sharp's nine assassins wreaked on the hapless archbishop in full view of his daughter is impossible to condone.

Neither Sharp nor his enemies showed much Christian charity or displayed any notion of religious tolerance. These values were in sadly short supply in seventeenth-century Scotland although they were exemplified by Sharp's colleague on the episcopal bench, the eirenic Robert Leighton, Bishop of Dunblane, whom we encountered at the beginning of the pilgrim way practising his sermons in The Study in Culross (see p. 44). In fact, it was Oliver Cromwell and his fellow English Independents who were the main champions of toleration and religious liberty in this troubled period, and who stood against the authoritarianism found in both Presbyterianism and Episco-palianism. That staunch Cromwellian, John Milton, was perhaps the father of religious toleration and liberty in Britain and its gradual spread through the eighteenth century owed as much to English Whigs and Dissenters as it did to the civilising effect of the Scottish Enlightenment.

The legacy of the Covenanters, and of the mythology which has surrounded them, lives on. It explains the lingering Scottish Presbyterian antipathy towards bishops and the perception of the Scottish Episcopal Church as 'the English Church'. This bloody and unedifying period in Scotland's religious history also explains the Kirk's antipathy towards the Stuarts and their Jacobite successors. When William of Orange and his wife Mary, daughter of James VII & II, were invited in 1689 by the English and Scottish parliaments to rule in place of her deposed Roman Catholic father, the Scottish bishops refused to give the new monarchs their allegiance while Presbyterians were happy to do so. As a result, Presbyterianism rather than Anglicanism/Episcopalianism became the established religion in Scotland. The Scottish Episcopalians, like the Roman Catholics, remained loyal to the Stuart Jacobite pretenders to the Crown against the Hanoverians for much of the eighteenth century and as a consequence found themselves cast into outer darkness. Later, as religious tolerance, or maybe religious indifference, came to prevail, the kind of ideological purity and defiant fighting spirit shown by the Covenanters found expression in other more political forms. Is there a link, I wonder, between Fife's Covenanters and its later Communists? Both were radical, anti-establishment, deeply ideological, convinced of the rightness of their cause and not prepared to compromise. Perhaps the twentieth-century Communist councillors of West Fife were the true heirs of the seventeenth-century Covenanters.

So there is much for modern pilgrims to reflect on as they cross that picturesque bridge in Ceres which Sharp may or may not have clattered over in his coach hours before meeting his brutal end. Magus Muir, where he was murdered, is not on the final stretch of the Fife Pilgrim Way, which forsakes the Bishop's Road in favour of a slightly more southerly route to St Andrews via Kinninmonth Hill, Drumcarro and Denhead. However, it can be seen from the top of Drumcarrow Crags, the high point before the final descent into St Andrews. It is well worth making the relatively short detour to view the site of this savage act carried out in the name of Christ on the old pilgrim way through Fife. It is a reminder of the terrible cost of religious authoritarianism, bigotry, fanaticism and intolerance, not least within the hearts of those professing the same Christian faith, and of the dire consequences when faith gets muddled with, or is hijacked by, politics and nationalism. The bloody deeds enacted along this stretch of the old pilgrim way seem directly contrary to Jesus's teaching about loving our enemies and turning the other cheek, although it is, of course, also the case that he made the rather chilling remark that he came to bring not peace but a sword and to set people against each other. Several of the Christians who walked the pilgrim paths of Fife in the seventeenth century seem to have followed those latter precepts with some alacrity.

Opposite
Magus Muir
Above:
Memorial
pyramid
Below:
Covenanters'
graves

PART 3
# Reaching the destination:
## St Andrews, the haunted city of relics and reformers

# 9
# St Andrews: the pilgrim city

It is well nigh impossible to enter St Andrews on foot nowadays other than alongside a golf course. Pilgrims arriving on the final leg of the Fife Pilgrim Way from Denhead walk along a wooded path beside the Duke's Course (so-called because it was opened by Prince Andrew, Duke of York, in 1995) before cutting through Craigtoun Park, down Lumbo Den and along the Lade Braes into the centre of the town. Those walking or cycling along the mediaeval pilgrim route from the north and west via Guardbridge have first the Eden and then the Old Course as their companions for the final five miles along the old railway track. The Fife Coastal Path skirts the edge of the Castle Course before descending down to the East Sands.

Previous spread
St Andrews
Cathedral

It is a reminder, if one were needed, that it is the religion of golf that lures most of the many visitors from around the world who flock to the town today. The little arched bridge over the Swilken Burn between the seventeenth and eighteenth fairways on the Old Course almost certainly attracts more veneration, and certainly more selfies, than the ruined cathedral, once the biggest and most imposing building in Scotland, and for many modern pilgrims the most sacred relics are to be found among the ancient putters, balls and silver trophies in the glass cabinets of the Royal and Ancient Clubhouse and the adjoining Museum of Golf.

But long before there were golf pilgrims, people were making their way to this isolated corner of the north-east Fife coast to venerate what they believed to be the relics of the apostle Andrew, the fisherman from Galilee who was one of the first disciples to be chosen by Jesus. For 400 years, from the late eleventh to the late fifteenth centuries, St Andrews was one of the main pilgrim destinations in Europe, being eclipsed possibly only by Rome, Santiago and Canterbury in terms of the numbers it attracted at the peak of its popularity. Even now, more than 500 years since the end of the great pilgrimage boom, the town centre still bears eloquent testimony to this period of its history. Uniquely in the United Kingdom, it is laid out specifically for the purposes of pilgrimage with two broad streets, North Street and South Street, running in parallel through the town to the cathedral, built to house St Andrew's shrine. They were designed as processional routes – at peak times a one-way system may have operated, with pilgrims walking down South Street to access the cathedral and then returning along North Street. Between these two broad avenues runs the narrower cobbled Market Street, so-called because it was where merchants set up their stalls to provide food and clothing and sell religious souvenirs.

Opposite
St Rule's Church
Tower

Pilgrimage was long St Andrews' *raison d'être* and substantial traces of several of the buildings associated with it can still be seen and visited around town. They include the prominent square tower and part of the nave of St Rule's Church, the first main repository of the apostle's relics; St Leonard's Chapel, tucked away in a courtyard off the end of South Street, which was attached to a pilgrim hospice; and the north chapel of Blackfriars, set up by the Dominicans along with other religious houses to cater for pilgrims, and now a picturesque ruin on South Street. The main gateways into the walled city through which pilgrims came – the West Port, which leads into South Street and the double-arched entrance from the harbour in the Pends – are still largely intact. The cathedral itself, which was among the largest in Europe, being 12 metres longer than the one at Santiago de Compostela and only 10 metres shorter than those at York and Durham, still dominates the eastern end of the town even in its present ruined state.

How did this remote and small coastal settlement on the edge of the North Sea become one of the major pilgrimage destinations of

Europe and the ecclesiastical capital of Scotland? The story is a fascinating one involving romantic legend, effective PR 'spin' by the Picts, Church politics and nationalistic sentiment in the new country of Scotland.

It was not until the late eleventh century that St Andrews acquired its present name. Its earliest recorded name seems to have been Muckross from the Gaelic *Mucrois*, meaning Boar's head or peninsula. It then became known as Cindrighmonaidh, later shortened to Kinrymont, a Pictish or Gaelic name which means the end of the king's headland or hill. This name points to a royal association and it is clear from other evidence that from at least the mid eighth century, and probably earlier, Kinrymont was the site of the palace of a Pictish king and an adjoining township, probably located on the headland above the harbour on what is now the site of the ruined church of St Mary on the Rock, also known as Kirkheugh. Later, the preface Kil was substituted, giving the name Kilrymont, and denoting a church or ecclesiastical settlement.

Like the rest of Pictish eastern Scotland both north and south of the River Tay, the area is likely first to have been evangelised by Christian monks from Ireland or from the Irish colony of Dal Riata in modern Argyll. Some sources suggest that the first missionary to come to Kinrymont was Kenneth or Cainnech of Aghaboe, a contemporary of Columba, who arrived from his monastery in Ossory in the south-east of Ireland around 570. This is an early date for missionary activity in the Pictish lands of eastern Scotland, which mostly seem not to have been generally evangelised until the seventh or eight centuries, although some archaeological finds in the Hallow Hill area, near where the Fife Pilgrim Way descends into the town, do suggest that there may have been Christians in the area as early as the sixth century. The first mention of Kenneth coming to *Cill Rig-Monaidh in Alba* is in the Martyrology of Oengus, which was written around 800, and the earliest documented description of a Christian community is in the Annals of Ulster, which record the death of an abbot called Tuathalan in the monastery there in 747. It is not certain where this early monastery was located. Fragments of Christian crosses, possibly dating from the eighth century although more likely to be from the ninth, found on the headland above the harbour now covered by the ruins of the Church of St Mary on the Rock suggest that this may have been the site of an early church in the area, and quite possibly of the monastery as well.

It was possibly around this time, in the mid to late eighth century, that the cult of Andrew, and perhaps his relics too, arrived in this corner of north-east Fife, although the two main accounts describing the arrival of his relics do not seem to have appeared until the eleventh or twelfth centuries. They both centre around a monk called Regulus, or Rule, who lived in the fourth or fifth century and was a native of Patras in Greece where, according to the Apocryphal Gospels, Andrew had been martyred around AD 65 by being bound and suspended on a diagonal cross on the orders of the Roman governor, Aegeas. One account suggests that Regulus was told in a dream around AD 350 to take some of the apostle's relics, of which he was apparently the keeper, to a place which would be shown to him. This was around the time that the Emperor Constantius II decided to move Andrew's body from Patras to Constantinople. The other foundation legend has Regulus being told to remove the relics to the 'outer limits of the empire' a hundred years later, during the reign of the Emperor Theodosius II. In both versions of the story, Regulus is described as arriving on the coast of north-east Fife, possibly as the result of a storm and shipwreck, bearing with him a tooth, arm bone, kneecap and three fingers of the apostle's right hand. There, at the gate called 'Matha', he apparently met the Pictish King Angus (or Oengus), who, the tale goes, joined him in making a seven-fold perambulation around the place carrying the apostle's relics above his head and subsequently 'assigned this spot to Almighty God and to the Holy Apostle St Andrew in perpetuity that it might be the chief and the mother of all the churches which are in the kingdom of the Picts'. The later twelfth-century foundation account goes on to record: 'To this city pilgrims flock, palmers from Jerusalem, Romans, Greeks, Armenians, Teutons,

Germans, Saxons, Danes, Galicians, French, Englishmen, Britons; men and women, rich and poor, the sick and the whole, lame and blind; with horses and carts the weak and crippled are carried, by God's glory and honour and the honour and glory of the saint and apostle Andrew, they come for cures' (Anderson 1980: 258–60).

In fact, it seems most likely that the story of Regulus bringing Andrew's relics to Fife was invented in the wake of the coming of the cult of the apostle to the Pictish realms of eastern Scotland from Northumbria in the eighth or ninth century. There was a widespread cult of Andrew across both eastern and western Christendom in the early Middle Ages and we know that it was particularly strong in the Anglian kingdom of Northumbria, where the important monastic church in Hexham was dedicated to him by St Wilfrid in the later seventh century. Acca, who served as abbot of St Andrew's monastery in Hexham and succeeded Wilfrid as bishop there in 709, is credited in at least one foundation legend with establishing an episcopal see at St Andrews around AD 732. He was a renowned collector of relics and may well have arrived in Fife with a relic or two of St Andrew, having possibly fled there after falling out with the Northumbrian king. Acca could have been welcomed by King Angus, referred to in the later version of the story as having met Regulus; this would have been an impossibility as he lived 400 years later than the monk, ruling from 730 until his death in 761. Angus may conceivably have been buried in the ornately decorated sarcophagus which is now on display in the cathedral museum, although it is probably of early ninth-century provenance and seems more likely to have contained the body of a later Pictish king, Constantine, who died in 820. Its decoration mixes biblical and Pictish symbolism and confirms the existence of a Christian Pictish royal settlement, incorporating a monastery, by this time. Angus appears to have succeeded King Nechthan who, according to Bede, made contact with the Roman Church in Northumbria, and it is quite possible that it is through the alliance he forged that the cult of Andrew became established in Kinrymont.

There was a second Pictish King Angus, who ruled from *c*. 820 to

*Opposite Window in St James' Church, St Andrews, showing St Rule bringing*

840, and some historians are inclined to the view that it was he rather than the earlier Angus who introduced the cult of St Andrew to Kinrymont and Fife. Several of the stories about King Angus portray him as being motivated by a promise of help against his enemies given in a dream by St Andrew. This dream is sometimes said to have been accompanied by the appearance of a white diagonal cross in the blue sky – one account mentions such an appearance on the eve of a battle against the Angles and Saxons in 832 in the vicinity of what is now Athelstaneford in East Lothian, supporting the theory that Angus II may have been the key figure in establishing the cult of Andrew. These stories, which provide an origin legend for the Saltire, or Scottish flag, need to be treated with some caution. Quite possibly modelled on the well-known story of the Emperor Constantine seeing a vision of the cross of Christ in the sky before the Battle of the Milvian Bridge in AD 312, they are almost certainly apocryphal and it was not until later in the Middle Ages that the association was firmly made between St Andrew, his diagonal cross and the Saltire as Scotland's national flag. A seal attached to a charter of 1190 which features a pair of bones crossed in an X shape hovering above St Rule's Church in St Andrews is thought to be the first depiction of the saltire motif.

Historians are generally agreed that the cult of St Andrew came to Kinrymont in the eighth or ninth centuries, probably under the patronage of either Angus I or Angus II, or perhaps with the latter king consolidating a cult established by his predecessor. Bones which could be presented as those of the saint were either discovered or brought to Kinrymont, not as in the foundation legend by Regulus travelling from the eastern Mediterranean, but rather by Acca or someone else coming from Northumbria. This dating ties in with what was happening across Europe at this time, when a general cult of the apostles and a movement to establish local links with their corporeal remains seems to have reached its height. The bones of St Mark are said to have been taken from Egypt to Venice in 828. At much the same time, around 830, the story first emerged of the body of St James turning up in a remote field in north-west Spain after drifting across the sea in a stone coffin. This apparent discovery led to the development of another great medieval city of pilgrimage, Santiago de Compostela. The emergence around the same time of the similarly far-fetched tale of St Regulus bringing relics of St Andrew to the east coast of Scotland seems less bizarre when seen in this wider European context.

It may well be significant that the cult of Andrew first seems to have emerged in north-east Fife during the period when the Picts of eastern Scotland were engaged in fierce battles with the Irish-speaking Gaels from Dal Riata for supremacy in what would later become the united Gaelic–Pictish kingdom of Scotland. There was no love lost between these two warring peoples. It is tempting to suggest that the legend of Regulus's arrival with Andrew's relics was seized upon, if not actually dreamed up, by the Picts to counter the Gaels and the strong popularity of their patron saint, Columba. The only way that Columba could be trumped was by producing an apostolic saint, and that agenda may have lain behind the promotion by the Picts of Andrew, who posthumously vied with Columba throughout the Middle Ages as favoured candidate for patron saint of the emerging Scottish nation.

The championship of Andrew was bound up with a vigorous campaign to have the Church at what was still known as Kinrymont recognised as having supremacy in Scotland. There was a significant and steady drift eastwards in the centre of Scottish ecclesiastical gravity in the early Middle Ages. The earliest powerhouse was Iona in the west in the seventh and eighth centuries. The focus moved to Dunkeld in Perthshire in 849 when Kenneth MacAlpine, the man credited – rightly or wrongly – with bringing together the Picts and the Gaels in the newly united kingdom of Scotland, moved Columba's relics there, apparently to prevent them being stolen by the Vikings on their ever more daring and damaging raids around the coast. The creation of the new kingdom of Scotland has traditionally been seen essentially as a result of the Gaels conquering the Picts. In fact, recent historians have suggested that there may have been a much more gradual process of assimilation and point out that MacAlpine himself was a Pict at least as much as he was a Gael. Was the gradual ecclesiastical ascendancy of what was to become St Andrews, which seems to have begun in the tenth century, an aspect of this process? There have been suggestions that Columba's relics were translated from Dunkeld to St Andrews to cement the latter's claim to be Scotland's spiritual heart, but I can find no evidence for this. Some sources suggest that the bishop of Kinrymont's position as the chief churchman in Scotland was recognised as early as around 906, but it is difficult to confirm or attest this assertion.

It is certainly clear that by the middle of the tenth century Kilrymont, as it was now increasingly being called, had become an important ecclesiastical centre and place of pilgrimage, with a significant monastic community. In 943 King Constantin mac Áeda abdicated his throne in order to become abbot there. Twenty years later, in 965, the first pilgrim whose name is recorded, an Irish prince called Áed, brother of the King of Tara, came to venerate Andrew's relics. There are several accounts of pilgrims coming to offer their devotions 'in the most famous house of the apostle Andrew' in the 1090s. By the late eleventh century the name St Andrews had been adopted, a large church had been built to house the supposed relics of the apostle and the number of pilgrims had increased sufficiently for Queen Margaret to establish the dedicated free ferry crossing for them over the Forth. Margaret herself seems to have been a frequent pilgrim to St Andrews and gave a jewelled cross for the altar of the principal church. She may also conceivably have helped to finance the building of a new church, which became known as St Rule's, to house Andrew's relics, although it does not seem to have been built until around 1120, more than two decades after her death. St Rule's Church was extended around 1140, during the reign of David I, who re-established it as a priory housing a chapter of Augustinian canons who were responsible for looking after the shrine, conducting worship and welcoming pilgrims. This move probably helped to consolidate both royal and ecclesiastical authority, which may have been somewhat challenged by the Culdee community which was in residence from the ninth century and ran a pilgrim hospice dedicated to St Leonard, which was made over to the Augustinian canons in 1144. Another pilgrim hospice, dedicated to St Nicholas and situated to the south of the town, seems to have catered especially for lepers.

In the late twelfth century accounts began to appear of apparently miraculous cures being experienced by those going on pilgrimage to St Andrews. A 'miracle of astonishing novelty' is recorded around 1190 in a Life of the seventh-century St Aebbe, founder abbess of the monastery at St Abb's near Coldingham on the Berwickshire coast: a cripple on his way to St Andrews happened to turn aside at Coldingham, where the local saint appeared to him in a dream and cured his ailment. It was, in fact, quite common in miracle stories for pilgrims heading to more famous shrines like St Andrews or Canterbury to be cured on the way at the shrine of a lesser-known saint. The fullest extant account of miracles being wrought at St Andrews comes from the *Chronica Gentis Scotorum* compiled by John of Fordun around 1380 and seems to be drawn from an account written around 1260: 'In that place by the touch of the relics, many astounding miracles were worked and are worked to this day, such had not until that day been seen or heard of in these islands since they embraced the faith; for instance, the blind from their mother's womb received their sight, the dumb were made to speak, the lame to walk, and all who piously bespoke the favour of the apostle (Andrew), were immediately, by God's mercy healed from the sickness that possessed them. As miracles were thus daily multiplied, people of all nations hastened thither with their gifts, clapping their hands, and humbly sending up boundless praises to God for so great a patron' (Skene 1871: 71–2).

It is not surprising, given this level of activity, that within twenty years of its enlargement, St Rule's Church appears to have become too small to house the growing number of pilgrims coming to venerate Andrew's relics and in 1160 construction began on the mighty cathedral, a project that took over 150 years to complete, with long delays caused by both financial and structural problems. Following the common pattern, the cathedral was built from east to west, with the Romanesque

Re-enactment
of St Andrews
Cathedral
consecration,
August 2018

eastern end, the choir and much of the nave being completed by the end of the twelfth century to allow veneration of the apostle's shrine, which was installed behind the high altar, and permit services to take place. A writ dating from the early thirteenth century describes a grant for the lighting of the cathedral paid from the proceeds of a brewery in Elie. Much of the west front was destroyed by a violent storm in the 1270s and had to be rebuilt in the early fourteenth century. The cathedral was finally consecrated in 1318 in the presence of seven bishops, fifteen abbots and King Robert the Bruce, who had four years earlier celebrated his victory over the English at Bannockburn. For Bruce, the cathedral was a thank-offering for the victory over the English at this battle. Legend has it that he rode up the nave on horse-back before placing a parchment on the High Altar expressing the nation's thanks to Andrew.

Bruce himself is said to have prayed on the eve of Bannockburn to Andrew as well as to 'the Scottish saints' – he also seems to have hedged his bets by praying to the English saint, Thomas of Canterbury, – and many of the Scottish soldiers wore the white cross of St Andrew on their tunics and invoked his protection before going into battle. Ironically, Bruce's great enemy in the Scottish Wars of Independence, the English King Edward I, known as the Hammer of the Scots, had himself come as a pilgrim to St Andrews during his attempt to conquer Scotland in 1304 and gave a gold jewel to adorn the casket containing the saint's arm. A number of English pilgrims are recorded as coming to St Andrews on the eve of the Wars of Independence in the 1270s and 1280s but, perhaps not surprisingly, few seem to have ventured there after Bannockburn.

Adjacent to the cathedral on its southern side extensive buildings were put up to house the growing community of Augustinian canons who sustained its liturgical life and ministered to pilgrims. The growing prestige and status of the bishops of St Andrews was reflected in another major building project which saw the erection in 1200 of the substantial episcopal palace, now known as the castle, on the rocky headland to the west of the cathedral.

The completion of the cathedral ushered in what were perhaps the boom years of pilgrimage to St Andrews. The processional routes of North and South Street were laid out, possibly modelled on those in Rome and Santiago, and several new churches and religious buildings sprang up in the expanding town. The Culdee community was reconstituted as a college of secular priests and given the Church of St Mary on the Rock, the foundations of which can still be clearly seen above the harbour, as a permanent home in 1248. Significantly, perhaps, it is located outside the city walls which were erected around 1300. The two major preaching orders of friars established houses in the town, the Dominicans at Blackfriars in South Street, where part of the chapel can still be seen, and the Franciscans in 1463 on the corner of Market Street and North Street, where the name Greyfriars Gardens is the only reminder of their presence. Together with the Augustinian canons based at the cathedral, these new arrivals were devoted to learning and scholarship, and maintained significant libraries; it was almost certainly to build on their teaching work that the university was founded by papal bull between 1410 and 1414, chiefly for the purpose of educating clergy. The parish church of the Holy Trinity was relocated from its original site next to the cathedral to its present position in the centre of town in 1412, and in 1460 the University Chapel of St Salvator was dedicated for worship, providing another imposing addition to the city's skyline of spires and towers which so impressed pilgrims as they gained their first glimpse of their destination. St Andrews came to be compared to Jerusalem, with its walls, gates and massive temple, especially as seen by pilgrims coming from the south, where it appeared to rise out of a hollow similar to the Valley of Kedron. Comparisons with Rome have also been made, notably by Ian Campbell, Professor of Architectural History and Theory at the University of Edinburgh, who has suggested that the architecture of the cathedral and the layout of St Andrews as a pilgrim city were deliberately modelled on St Peter's and the streets leading to it. He points out that one of the foundation legends describes St Andrews as an apostolic see and 'the second Rome' (Campbell 2013: 21).

The cathedral was not without its problems. In 1378 a serious fire destroyed the roof. In 1389 the prior was stabbed to death by a fellow canon on the night stair leading up to the dormitory (see p. 110). In 1410 a severe storm brought the south gable crashing down through the refectory and in 1421 a fight broke out among the clergy, a reminder that, then as now, all was not necessarily sweetness and light in the relationships between fellow Christians. However, these setbacks did not seriously affect its appeal as a destination for pilgrims. By the middle of the fifteenth century the population of St Andrews had probably reached around 3,000, including several hundred monks and clergy. Nearly all of the city's inhabitants, whether lay or clerical, were involved in some way in supporting the booming business of pilgrimage. St Andrew's relics were housed in a richly decorated coloured enamel reliquary, or morbrac, in a chapel at the east end of the cathedral behind the high altar. To cater for the growing number who came to venerate the relics, several pilgrim routes were established across Fife in addition to the main one coming from North Queensferry via Dunfermline, Scotlandwell, Markinch, Kennoway and Ceres. A longer ferry crossing across the Forth linked North Berwick and Earlsferry. Pilgrims from west and north Scotland converged at a large holding station which was built at Guardbridge before crossing the River Eden and walking into the city along the route of the present cycle track (and old railway line) from Leuchars. Several pilgrims came from continental Europe. In 1319 Walter Maisiere of Kortrijk in what is now Belgium was directed to make a pilgrimage to St Andrews as a penance for assaulting his wife. In 1325 John Host from Flanders was granted safe conduct to make a pilgrimage to St Andrews in fulfilment of a vow. In 1333 Wille Bondolf, a cleric in Dunkirk who had killed a local man, well known for his violent and provocative behaviour, in self-defence, was brought before the judicial authorities of St Omer and sentenced to embark on a pilgrimage to St Andrews alone and on foot as an 'expiatory trial of contrition and endurance'. In his *Scotichronicon*, written around 1440, Walter Bower noted that 'The boastful Frank and the bellicose Norman, the Flemish weaver, the

Opposite
Reproduction
of morbrac,
St Andrews
Museum

213

uncouth Teuton, the Englishman, the German, the Hollander, strangers from Poitou and quarrelsome folk from Angers, men who drank the waters of the Rhine and the Rhone or the lordly Tiber, they all come here to seek the help of St Andrew.'

As in the case of Bondolf, some pilgrims came to St Andrews as penitents, serving out sentences from ecclesiastical courts for crimes that they had committed. Others came to give thanks to God for some deliverance, to seek healing, or perhaps simply out of a sense of adventure. Pilgrimage also provided just about the only opportunity for people living in the Middle Ages to take a break from work and escape the confines of home. As pilgrims they met new friends and travelled, perhaps for the only time in their lives, to new places. Many would have journeyed for several weeks, if not months, and timed their arrival in St Andrews to coincide with one of the great festivals or feast days when there were processions and celebrations throughout the town. The main pilgrim season started with the celebration of the Coming of the Relics on 6 February (the feast day of St Merinus, who was credited in some stories with accompanying Andrew's relics to Scotland) and ended on St Andrew's Day (30 November). Numerous other festivals and holy days were celebrated in between with processions, bell ringing, music, feasting and entertainments. The huge cost of maintaining the cathedral led to indulgences being sold to pilgrims coming on special days. As early as 1290 the Pope had granted a special indulgence for those visiting on the feast of the Assumption (15 August). The need for funds became urgent following the fire in 1378 and the collapse of the south gable in 1410 and several papal indulgences were granted to raise money for repairs during the fifteenth century, including two major ones granted in 1473 and 1487 to those visiting the cathedral on the feast of St Michael (29 September). On these and other holy days, processions through the town were led by the Augustinian canons with the morbrac, which is said to have weighed around a third of a ton, being carried in procession on its bier and held high under a canopy by twenty-four carefully chosen strong men. Pilgrims followed the relics in and out of the great west door of the cathedral. On other occasions, they would probably have entered by the north porch door in the nave and received communion at one of the numerous side altars. In addition to venerating the relics and participating in services in the many places of worship around the town, pilgrims also had plenty of opportunities for retail therapy, with stalls selling souvenirs, such as the pilgrim badges in the shape of Andrew's diagonal cross which have been found across Britain and beyond.

Meanwhile, Andrew himself was gradually achieving ascendancy over Columba in the long posthumous battle between them as to who would be patron saint of Scotland. A significant indicator of his rising status was the production of a great seal in 1286 following the death of King Alexander III, where for the first time the figure of the king was replaced by that of the saint on his diagonal cross with the legend *Andreas dux esto Scotis compatriotis* (Andrew be leader of your Scottish compatriots). The wars of independence with England in the late thirteenth and early fourteenth centuries consolidated his position as the Scots' patron saint. A key point of Scottish propaganda, directed at successive popes in an attempt to gain their backing for claims of independence against the English kings, was that God had especially favoured the Scots by procuring their conversion through the relics of Andrew at a date long before the conversion of the English. Andrew was taken up as a national champion in disputes with the English, not least in the ecclesiastical sphere over English claims that Scotland fell within the jurisdiction of the Archbishop of York. This was a major bone of contention with the Scottish clergy, who appealed to Pope John XXII in the Declaration of Arbroath of 1320, arguing that the Scots were a distinct people who had long enjoyed the protection of an apostle.

Andrew's cross was increasingly employed through the fourteenth century as a national symbol in opposition to the cross of St George. An act of the Scottish Parliament in 1385 explicitly called on Scottish soldiers to wear the Saltire emblem in battles against the English. Andrew also started appearing on coins in this period. All of this, of course, helped the claims of the bishops of St Andrews to supremacy in the Scottish Church although it took them a long time to achieve the metropolitan status that they craved. Even if they were de facto recognised as pre-eminent, it was not until 1472 that Patrick Graham, Bishop of St Andrews, became Scotland's first archbishop. Andrew's position as the leading saint of Scotland was confirmed in the Aberdeen Breviary in 1510, where he was referred to as *Scotorum sanctissimus patronus*, to be honoured in all Scottish churches with a weekly commemoration. The official 'establishment' candidate for the role of patron saint, championed by the ecclesiastical and political authorities, had finally triumphed over his Gaelic rival.

Andrew has left his visual mark on the town that still bears his name. He appears, among other places, in a little niche on the wall above J & G Innes' stationery shop in Church Street, in a panel high up on the tower of the Town Hall and in a stained glass window in St James's Church on the Scores. The most imposing depiction of the apostle is a statue made in 1850 to adorn the Edinburgh head office of an insurance company. A copy of François Duquesnoy's seventeenth-century statue in the transept of St Peter's Basilica in Rome, it was given to St Andrews University in 1964 and for many years languished among overhanging bushes in the car park of the Botanic Gardens off the Canongate. It is currently undergoing restoration prior to being moved to a more visible and central location, initially in the grounds of the University Museum and ultimately close to the ruins of Blackfriars Chapel in South Street, where it will greet pilgrims completing the Fife Pilgrim Way.

Ironically, just as Andrew and St Andrews had finally won their long struggle for pre-eminence, thanks to a combination of romantic myth-making, nationalistic sentiment and exercise of the dark arts of public relations, the pilgrimage boom was coming to an end. There were various reasons for this, including an overall decline in the cults of apostles, which were giving way to devotion to the Virgin Mary, and also a general downturn in pilgrimage and the appeal of cathedral shrines across western Europe. In the case of St Andrews, the university became a rival attraction to the cathedral and began to draw more

Opposite Images of St Andrew Left: On wall in Church Street Right: Copy of statue in St Peter's, Rome

people to the city. When Bishop Henry Wardlaw asked the Pope to grant an indulgence to finance the building of a bridge across the River Eden in 1419 (which still stands today next to the modern road bridge) after fifteen clerics were drowned trying to make the crossing, he did not mention the needs of pilgrims but rather the importance of securing the safe passage of students to St Andrews. In 1512 St Leonard's Hospice was converted from a pilgrim hospital into student accommodation. The foundation charter of the new St Leonard's College that year noted that 'miracles and pilgrimages had in a measure ceased so that the hospital was without pilgrims' and tried to put a positive spin on this development by adding that it had come about because 'the Christian faith, firmly rooted in the land, no longer needed such support'. This document provides interesting evidence that students were coming to supplant pilgrims as the main group of visitors requiring accommodation in the town – so they remain today with increasing numbers of student residences being built to house the 9,000 or so undergraduates and postgraduates now studying in the university.

It is clear that pilgrimage was already in marked decline fifty years or so before the event which is usually blamed for killing it off, the Scottish Reformation of 1560. Ironically, the last recorded visitor to the relics of St Andrew was a Lutheran agent, Magnus Wagner, who posed as a pilgrim in 1553 in order to investigate the shrine and acquire some manuscripts. But if the Protestant Reformers cannot be held responsible for ending St Andrews' original *raison d'être*, they certainly changed both the physical and spiritual landscape of the town in ways which have left profound marks to this day.

# 10
# St Andrews, the Reformation city

St Andrews played a central role in the bitter religious struggles which engulfed Scotland in the first half of the sixteenth century and which led to the movement known as the Reformation. This was partly because of the fact that it was effectively the headquarters of the Scottish Church, the seat of the Cardinal Archbishop who presided over that Church and the site of its greatest and grandest cathedral. It was also because of the particularly strong influence that the ideas and teachings of continental Reformers like Martin Luther and Jean Calvin exerted on students and teachers in the university. Four men were publicly burned to death in the town for their Protestant beliefs and the event generally seen as kick-starting the Scottish Reformation took part in the town kirk when John Knox preached a sermon which so inflamed his congregation, which included the town's magistrates and baillies, that they resolved to tear down the statues and stained-glass windows in the church and the cathedral. It is significant and appropriate that St Andrews was the only place in the United Kingdom designated a Reformation City in 2017 by the Community of Protestant Churches in Europe as part of the commemoration of the 500th anniversary of the start of the Protestant Reformation.

The three main colleges of St Andrews University, St Salvator's, St Leonard's and St Mary's, were founded in the later fifteenth and early sixteenth centuries to defend Catholic orthodoxy and train clergy for the medieval Church. St Salvator's, founded in 1450 by Bishop

James Kennedy, remained broadly orthodox and loyal to the teachings of the Church. St Mary's College was founded as the New College or College of the Assumption of the Blessed Virgin Mary in 1538 by Archbishop James Beaton on the site of or close to an older foundation, St John's College, which had been established in 1418 but gone into decline. A document signed by James V in 1539 described its purpose as being 'the teaching and instruction of our lieges in the Catholic faith, the opposing of heresy, administration of justice, instruction of able men in culture, science and policy within our realm and for maintaining divine worship by daily prayers'. James Beaton, his nephew Cardinal David Beaton and his successor Archbishop John Hamilton sought to make St Mary's College a centre for moderate reformed Catholicism to counter the heretical teachings of more radical reformers which were beginning to seep in from continental Europe. It was dedicated to a revival of learning on the humanist principles expounded by Erasmus, himself an Augustinian canon like those in St Andrews Priory, and the continental trilingual model emphasising knowledge of Latin, Greek and Hebrew. Had its reforming ethos begun somewhat earlier or been more wholehearted, it might have helped to stem the tide of anti-Catholic sentiment coming from the continent; this was especially affecting students and staff in St Leonard's College, which had been founded as 'The College of Poor Clerks of the Church of St Andrews' in 1512 by Alexander Stewart, Archbishop of St Andrews and John Hepburn, Prior of St Andrews, taking over the buildings of St Leonard's Hospital and Church. But reform from within the Catholic Church, as attempted at St Mary's College in the 1540s and 1550s, was too little and too late. Continental Reformed ideas, attacking the perceived corruption, idolatry, superstition and authority of the late medieval Catholic Church, were widely taken up in St Leonard's College and it was from there that many of Scotland's early Protestants came.

An early indication of the movement of reform sweeping in from the continent and also a harbinger of the terrible fate that was to befall exponents of religious reform and blacken the streets of St Andrews with the charred remains of martyrs came in 1433, with the burning at the stake near the market cross of Pavel Kravar (Paul Craw), a follower of the Bohemian reformer, Jan Hus. Craw, who had studied medicine in Paris and taken up a position at the University of Prague, seems to have come to St Andrews in the hope of finding sympathisers with his reformed ideas among those in the university influenced by the teaching of the fourteenth-century English reformer, John Wycliffe. Like Wycliffe and Hus, Craw attacked the wealth and power of the papacy and clergy, the Catholic doctrine of transubstantiation in the Mass and the practice of indulgences, and argued for the translation of the Bible from Latin into the language of the people. Shortly after arriving, he was arrested on the orders of Bishop Henry Wardlaw and, following interrogation by Laurence of Lindores, Abbot of Scone and the official inquisitor, he was sentenced to death by burning for heresy. According to a later account a brass ball was stuffed into his mouth to prevent him addressing the considerable crowd which gathered to witness his agonising end in the market square. In 2015, the 600th anniversary of the martyrdom of Jan Hus, a blue memorial plaque was erected close to the site of Craw's death. It was dedicated in 2016 by the Czech ambassador to the United Kingdom. With inscriptions in English and Czech, the language which the Hussites used in preference to Latin for their religious observances, it incorporates the symbol of a chalice, signifying the Hussites' belief in communion in both kinds (bread and wine) in contrast to the medieval Catholic practice of offering the laity only bread.

As is well known, Scotland, and the Church of Scotland in particular, ultimately drew more in terms of theology, doctrines and forms of Church government and polity from the French Geneva-based reformer, Jean Calvin, than it did from the more conservative figure of Martin Luther, the other founding father of the European Reformation. However, the influence of Luther was hugely important in the early years of the spread of Protestant ideas from the continent. Luther's critique of medieval Catholicism and his strong assertion of the doctrine of justification by personal faith alone, without recourse to works, the accumulation of merit or the activities of the Church, first came into Scotland from Germany and the Low Countries in the form of literature which circulated particularly in the east coast burghs. St Andrews, with its own harbour and proximity to the major port of Dundee, became one of the main entry points for this 'heretical' literature from the continent and a centre for the reception and transmission of Luther's ideas.

The first and best-known St Andrews Protestant martyr was Patrick Hamilton, who was also the first Protestant martyr in Scotland. He was born near Glasgow around 1504 and studied at the University of Paris, where he came into contact with the humanist teachings of Erasmus. In 1523 he enrolled as a student at St Leonard's College in St Andrews University, where he probably first encountered Luther's writings, and he became a priest in 1526. His open support for the banned teachings of Luther, notably the idea of justification by faith alone, brought him into direct conflict with James Beaton, Archbishop of St Andrews. Hamilton retreated to Germany in 1527, where he visited Wittenberg and Marburg, both leading centres of Lutheranism, and wrote a book with a strongly Lutheran slant. Back in Scotland the following year he was summoned before Beaton on charges of heresy, found guilty and slowly burned to death at the stake on 29 February 1528 at the age of just twenty-four. John Knox painted a graphic pen picture of Hamilton's martyrdom as the starting point of his book on the Reformation in Scotland:

> The innocent servant of God being bound to the stake in the midst of some coals, some timber, and other matter appointed for the fire, a train of powder was made and set on fire, which neither kindled the wood nor yet the coals. And so remained the appointed to death in torment, till men ran to the Castle again for more powder, and for wood more able to take fire; which at last being kindled, with loud voice he cried: 'Lord Jesus, receive my spirit! How long shall darkness overwhelm this Realm? How long wilt Thou suffer this tyranny of men?'

The fire was slow, and therefore was his torment the more. But most of all was he grieved by certain wicked men, amongst whom Alexander Campbell, the Black Friar, was principal, who continually cried, 'Convert, heretic! Call upon our Lady! Say Salve Regina.' To whom he answered, 'Depart and trouble me not, ye messengers of Satan.' But while the aforesaid Friar still roared, one thing in great vehemency Master Patrick said unto him: 'Wicked man, thou knowest the contrary, and the contrary to me thou hast confessed. I appeal thee before the Tribunal Seat of Jesus Christ!' After which and other words, which well could not be understood for the tumult, and the vehemency of the fire, this witness of Jesus Christ got victory, after long sufferance, the last of February, in the year of God, 1528.

Hamilton's death provoked a considerable reaction. Alexander Alesius, an Augustinian canon of the cathedral who had been one of those responsible for prosecuting him during his trial, was so affected by his death that he renounced Catholicism and went into exile in Germany as a Protestant reformer. He never returned to Scotland. According to John Knox, James Lyndsay, an adviser to James Beaton, counselled the archbishop against any further public burnings and suggested that if he did insist on putting any more heretics to death, 'let them be burnt in underground cellars, for the reek of Master Patrick Hamilton has infected as many as it blew upon'. Despite this warning, Beaton meted out a similar fate on the second St Andrews Protestant martyr, Henry Forrest, a Benedictine friar from Linlithgow who was burned to death in 1533 for possessing a New Testament in English and affirming that Patrick Hamilton had died as a martyr and that his doctrines were true. Forrest was burned outside the north entrance of the cathedral, which looks out over the harbour and the sea, so, it is said, that the smoke from his pyre could be seen right up the coast of Angus and serve as a warning to any would-be Reformers there.

The third St Andrews Protestant martyr, almost as well known as Hamilton, was George Wishart, an austere, saintly figure who became

Scotland's first itinerant expository preacher. Born in 1513 in Auchenblae in Kincardineshire, the son of the Lord Justice Clerk of Scotland, he went to the University of Aberdeen, served as a schoolmaster in Montrose and then began his preaching career at Bristol, where he was arraigned for heresy. He went as an exile to the continent, first to Germany and then to Switzerland, where he imbibed the doctrines of the Swiss Reformers. He returned to Scotland in 1543 and embarked on an extensive preaching tour where he expounded such Reformed principles as justification by faith, the priesthood of all believers and reading the Bible in the vernacular. Arrested on the orders of Cardinal David Beaton, who had succeeded his uncle, James, as Archbishop of St Andrews, he was imprisoned in the castle which served as the bishop's palace and condemned to be hanged and burned to death as a heretic just outside it on 1 March 1546. According to George Buchanan, the Protestant historian and humanist scholar, on the morning of his execution Wishart was invited into the chamber of the commandant of the castle who, by some accounts, was sympathetic to his ideas, and offered a last breakfast. Wishart asked if he could bless the food and proceeded to give a half-hour discourse on the Lord's Supper. He then broke the bread and passed it round with a goblet of wine, which he had also blessed. This action, which is generally regarded to have been the first Reformed celebration of the sacrament of communion in Scotland, is the subject of a painting of 1853 by Sir William Orchardson, 'Wishart's Last Exhortation'.

Opposite
'Wishart's Last
Exhortation'

As in the case of Hamilton, John Knox provided a dramatic account of Wishart's death. Noting that Cardinal Beaton was so concerned that Wishart's many friends and supporters might seek to rescue him that he commanded a contingent of gunners to stand beside their weapons until after his burning, Knox reported that Wishart was led out of the castle with his hands behind his back, a rope around his neck and an iron chain around his waist. Coming out into the street outside, which was thronged with people, he prayed three times: 'O Thou Saviour of the World, have mercy upon me! Father of Heaven, I commend my spirit into Thy holy hands.' Then he turned to the

assembled crowd and said: 'I beseech you, Christian Brethren and Sisters, be not offended at the Word of God, for the affliction and torments which ye see prepared for me. But I exhort you, love the Word of God and suffer patiently, and with a comfortable heart, for the Word's sake, which is your undoubted salvation and everlasting comfort.' Having affirmed that 'I know surely that my soul shall sup with my Saviour this night', he then prayed for those who had accused him, saying: 'I beseech Thee, Father of Heaven, forgive them that have of any ignorance, or else of any evil mind, forged lies upon me. I forgive them with all my heart. I beseech Christ to forgive them that have condemned me to death this day ignorantly.' The hangman then fell upon his knees and said: 'Sir, I pray you, forgive me, for I am not guilty of your death.' Wishart told him to approach and kissed his cheek, saying: 'Lo! Here is a token that I forgive thee. My heart, do thine office!' Finally, in Knox's words, 'the trumpet sounding, he was put upon the gibbet and hanged, and there burnt to powder. When the people beheld the great tormenting of that innocent, they might not withhold from piteous mourning and complaining of the innocent lamb's slaughter' (Knox 1982: 64–5). Cardinal Beaton watched the entire proceedings from an upstairs window in the castle.

The fourth and final St Andrews Protestant martyr and the last to die for his faith in sixteenth-century Scotland, Walter Milne, was a former priest at Lunan in Angus who was tortured and burned to death at the age of eighty-two in 1558 for holding the Mass to be idolatrous and for supporting clerical marriage and private preaching. He was burned outside the west gate of the cathedral, probably on what is now the cobbled pavement outside Dean's Court, formerly the residence of the Archdeacon of St Andrews and now a university hall of residence for postgraduates.

At the heart of what led these Protestant Reformers to face death at the hands of their fellow Christians was their belief in justification by faith alone. This was the crux of Luther's theology, a breakthrough which ended years of anguished agonising about his own salvation. It came to him while he was reading the first chapter of St Paul's Epistle to the Romans. He became convinced that salvation is not dependent on our own merits or on any works that the Church does – rather God in his infinite mercy pardons our sins and welcomes us to eternal life with him, offering a new start and complete forgiveness – all that we have to do is to respond in faith.

In the eyes of its opponents, the medieval Catholic Church preached and practised a very different view of salvation, which rested on the power of priests, on performing works to gain merit and obtaining indulgences to reduce the time spent in Purgatory, that intermediate state between this world and the next, where souls would be purged before the Last Judgement. The Reformers preached the priesthood of all believers and the centrality of faith alone in the attainment of salvation and eternal life.

It was not just Protestants who were put to death in St Andrews during this bloody and unedifying period of Scottish history. On 29 May 1546 Cardinal David Beaton was stabbed to death by eighteen Protestant nobles who stormed his palace in the castle following the death of George Wishart. Their leader, Norman Leslie, was a local man, being laird of the Castle of Tacis which stood in Teasses Den just south of the Waterless Road as it comes into Ceres; his wife, Isobel Lindsay, was from Struthers Castle. According to A.H. Millar's 1895 *History of Fife*, one of Isobel's five sisters somewhat ironically became the wife of one of Cardinal Beaton's eight children by his long-term mistress Marion Ogilvy, but I can find no record of this in the Lindsay family tree (Millar 1895: I: 146). The cardinal's body was suspended by a sheet attached to his arm and leg and hung out from the window from which he had watched Wishart's burning just two months earlier. The nobles occupied the castle for over a year, being joined shortly after Easter 1547 by John Knox as tutor to their children. He taught them Latin and the catechism in the chapel, on the first floor of the castle's eastern front overlooking where Wishart had been burned. Asked by the Protestant occupiers to be their preacher, he initially hesitated at such a responsibility but felt that he could not resist what he took to be a call from God to be 'a witness, minister and preacher'.

So it was that his preaching ministry began in St Andrews. He preached his first-ever sermon in Holy Trinity Parish Church early in the summer of 1547, attacking the papacy and the Roman Catholic Church. At the invitation of John Winram, subprior of the cathedral, who was himself sympathetic to the Reformers and subsequently converted from Catholicism to Protestantism in 1559, Knox regularly preached on weekdays in Holy Trinity Church, expounding Reformed doctrines, and was allowed to administer the Lord's Supper on Reformed lines. Ironically, the same pulpit was occupied on Sundays by Catholic preachers, led by Dean John Annand, Principal of St Leonard's College, fulminating against the Protestants.

Throughout the period of its Protestant occupation, the castle was besieged in a somewhat desultory manner by troops under the command of James Hamilton, Second Earl of Arran, Governor of Scotland and regent for the infant Queen Mary. He was constrained in his efforts, not least because his own son and heir was one of the prisoners held by the Protestant nobles. An attempt by the besiegers to topple the castle wall by undermining it was foiled by the occupants digging a counter-mine. Throughout the first twelve months of the siege, those inside the castle seem to have been allowed to come and go, allowing Knox to carry on with his preaching at Holy Trinity. However, the situation changed dramatically in July 1547 with the arrival of a fleet of twenty-one French galleys, sent on the orders of the regents. They landed fourteen cannons, which were placed on top of the cathedral towers and St Salvator's College. On 31 July salvos from these cannons, beginning at four in the morning and continuing for six hours, inflicted considerable damage and caused the Protestant occupants to surrender on condition that their lives were spared. Many, including Knox, were captured by the French and became galley slaves. The castle was then destroyed and its walls demolished.

John Knox spent nineteen months as a galley slave, an experience from which his health never recovered. He was forced to make two journeys to the waters off the east coast of Scotland – on the second one in the summer of 1548, he fell seriously ill and thought he was

Opposite
Holy Trinity
Church, west
front

229

dying. His galley lay off St Andrews and one of his friends raised him so that he could see the shoreline and recognise it. He replied, 'Yes, I know it well; for I see the steeple of that place, where God first in public opened my mouth to his glory, and I am fully persuaded, how weak that ever I now appear, that I shall not depart this life till that my tongue shall glorify his godly name in the same place' (Dawson 2015: 56–7). Eventually freed in April 1549 thanks to diplomatic representations from the English Government, he found refuge first in England under Edward VI and then in exile in Geneva. He returned to Scotland in 1555 to take an active role in the escalating conflict between Catholics (supported by the regent and by France) and Protestants (supported by England) in what were to become known as the Wars of the Congregations. St Andrews became the headquarters of the Protestant cause and the base of the Protestant Lords of the Congregation who established worship on the principles established by Jean Calvin in Geneva.

Knox returned to preach in St Andrews in the early summer of 1559, fulfilling the vow he had made as a galley slave. Ignoring a threat from Archbishop Hamilton that 'a dozen culverings [guns] should light upon his nose' if he preached there, in a series of sermons from the pulpit of Holy Trinity Knox laid into what he took to be the idolatry and corruption at the heart of the Catholic Church. On 11 June he took as his text Jesus's dispersal of the money-changers from the temple and encouraged his congregation in a similar way to purge the church and cathedral of idolatrous ornaments. A contemporary account records that 'the sermon was scarcely down, when they fell to work to purge the kirk and break down the altars and images and all kinds of idolatry'(Laing 1844: 58). It also suggests that the congregation may have gone on to the cathedral where they removed idolatrous statues and furniture and made a bonfire of them on the spot where Milne had been burned to death a year earlier. Whether, as local legend suggests, the congregation did indeed storm out of the church en masse following Knox's fiery sermon, rampage along South Street and attack the cathedral, smashing stained-glass windows, statues and other perceived idols, is not absolutely certain. The idea that Knox's sermon directly inspired an immediate orgy of destruction is perpetuated in a tourist leaflet designed for visitors to St Andrews in 2018 and 2019 which states that Blackfriars Chapel in South Street 'suffered at the hands of the mob after John Knox's sermon on the 11th June 1559, who pulled it down' (*Explore St Andrews* published by scottishpass.com). In fact, it seems more likely that it was only objects in Holy Trinity that were initially destroyed, with the magistrates, provost and baillies of the town subsequently agreeing to 'remove all monuments of idolatry, which they also did with expedition' as Knox reported. However they happened, these acts of iconoclasm have often been taken as marking the start of the Scottish Reformation. Archbishop Hamilton fled to Falkland and the regent (Mary of Guise) sent troops under a French commander to Cupar in support of him and the Catholic cause. Protestants from across north-east Fife massed on the Hill of Tarvit and frightened the regent's troops into signing a truce. The Lords of the Congregation, with Knox as their military chaplain, swept through central Scotland, taking Perth and Stirling and marching into Edinburgh.

Although the Protestant side seemed to be in the ascendant, the outcome of the Wars of the Congregation was not immediately certain. In January 1560 the regent's forces were going through Fife burning the homes of Protestant lairds and came within six miles of the Protestant stronghold of St Andrews when they heard that an English fleet had sailed into the Forth to support the Protestants. This caused them to retreat, as they did not want to be trapped in Fife. The arrival of the English fleet, which was followed by an English army marching into Scotland, marked the turning point in the Wars of the Congregation, decisively tipping it in the Protestants' favour. Aided by the English, the Protestants won the battle with the French-supported regent and Catholic party, and in 1560 the Scottish Parliament renounced the authority of the Pope and declared Scotland a Protestant and Presbyterian nation.

St Andrews was in the forefront of the movement which established the Scottish Church on Reformed principles. Knox stayed in the city to make it a bastion and banner of Reformed ecclesiology, worship and discipline, organising the Church on the Genevan model based on a Kirk Session exercising order and discipline, an emphasis on preaching the Word and a Reformed celebration of the sacrament of communion. The English Admiral Winter and other naval officers attended Holy Trinity, where Knox had established himself as de facto minister, to hear him preach. Knox remained there until 1561, when Christopher Goodman took over as the first 'settled minister' of St Andrews. By 1564 the town kirk's elders were congratulating themselves that St Andrews possessed 'ane perfyt reformed kyrk' with 'the sacraments deuly ministrat, all thingis done in the kyrk by comely order establesched, and disciplyn used' (Dawson 2015: 197).

If the sacking of the cathedral seems an unjustifiably violent and barbaric action for Christians to engage in, we should remember that the four Protestant martyrs had all been tried within its walls and forced to stand in the pulpit to defend themselves and face their sentences of death for heresy. It is perhaps not surprising in these circumstances if a bonfire of some of its wooden statues and paintings was lit on the exact spot where Milne had so recently been burned to death. The cathedral ceased to be a place of worship from 1560 and the priory was closed down, although the chapter of Augustinian canons continued to exist for some time. At least fifteen of the regular canons became ministers in the new Reformed Kirk, suggesting more continuity between the old Catholic and new Protestant faith than might be guessed from the rather partisan accounts that we have of this period from protagonists on both sides. Only those cathedrals which were also parish churches, like Glasgow, were allowed to continue in use as places of worship. St Andrews had its own parish church, Holy Trinity, so the cathedral fell into ruin. It had always been unstable and it may be that long-standing structural weaknesses contributed as much if not more to its fairly rapid physical disintegration as did the activities of Protestant iconoclasts. It is likely that the lead from the roof was one of the first materials to be removed from the building, being then as now of considerable value. This would have let the rain in and caused significant damage. It is also clear that relatively soon after its closure as a place of worship, stones were removed for building work around the town.

What is something of a mystery is the fate of the morbrac containing the supposed relics of St Andrew. Presumably it would have been the object that the Augustinian canons would have been most keen to save when the cathedral was stripped of its supposedly idolatrous contents, which may, as noted, have been a gradual rather than a sudden process. Tantalisingly, and somewhat curiously, there is no record of what became of it. Was it secreted somewhere in the grounds or the vicinity of the priory, or was it spirited away to some other more distant place of safety? No one seems to know. Many years ago I had a knock on the door of my study at St Mary's College. A group of parishioners from Portmoak, which lies near the Fife/Kinross border on the east side of Loch Leven overlooking St Serf's Island, claimed that local legend suggested that St Andrew's relics were removed there and put in a chapel, the site of which is now in the middle of Portmoak Airfield, the base of the Scottish Gliding Union. They asked me if I knew anything about this story. I took it up with various Catholic historians but no one I consulted has been able to verify it. Maybe the relics, like the Holy Grail, lie somewhere waiting to be discovered!

Perhaps just as much of a mystery in a different way is how quickly and apparently seamlessly, given the violence and animosity which had led up to it, St Andrews switched from being Catholic to Protestant. For all the Reforming influences through St Leonard's College, the four martyrs and the commanding figure of Knox, it was, after all, the headquarters of the Catholic Church in Scotland, the seat of its archbishop and packed with Catholic clergy and monks serving the cathedral, religious houses and churches. Bess Rhodes points out in her thesis on Reformation St Andrews 'in the spring of 1559 St Andrews was still a functioning Catholic city. By the end of the summer the burgh had become a bastion of the Protestant cause' (Rhodes 2013:

233

85). In their recent book on medieval St Andrews, Michael Brown and Katie Stevenson point to the rapidity and decisiveness of what happened in 1559 and suggest that it perhaps owed something to local political, social and economic tensions between Church and community as well as more specifically religious and theological considerations:

> The preaching of John Knox in Holy Trinity Church on 11 and 14 June marked the beginning of a planned attack on the institutions of Scotland's ecclesiastical capital. This change altered all aspects of the medieval city. The archbishop was forced to flee, leaving his castle occupied by the reformers. The friaries were sacked and partially demolished. The cathedral priory was also attacked and 'put down' and the books and sculptures of the community destroyed. The relics which had formed the centre of devotion at the site for eight centuries were removed or destroyed. The life of the Augustinian house effectively ended. Over the next few years, the possessions and revenues of these houses in and beyond St Andrews were assigned to, or uplifted by, other individuals or bodies. This change was not just an external assault. Its architect, James Stewart, the bastard son of James V, held the office of prior of St Andrews. Moreover, the attacks had support from a sizable group of St Andrews burgesses, whose motives may, in part, reflect tensions between the urban community and its overlords. For St Andrews, however, the events of 1559 mark the end not just of its pre-Reformation history, but of its history as a major centre of power and spirituality. (Brown & Stevenson 2017: 18)

It is certainly true that John Knox made St Andrews both the cradle and the heart of the Scottish Reformation and changed the physical as well as the spiritual face of the city as a result. Significantly, he returned at the end of his life to the town and church that he loved. He spent much of his last eighteen months in St Andrews, preaching occasionally in Holy Trinity, continuing to stir up controversy and renewing old animosities with those whom he felt were still too Catholic and had not espoused Reform. He died in Edinburgh, where he is buried rather ingloriously under parking lot no. 23 behind St Giles' Cathedral. There have been several reported sitings of Knox's ghost in the streets of St Andrews. A university lecturer claimed to have seen him dressed in a Geneva gown and with an armed bodyguard in North Street one night, and in the early 1960s a young couple reported seeing him apparently watching the castle.

Visiting in 1773, Dr Johnson found St Andrews to be a place of ruins and had no hesitation in blaming Knox for this state of affairs: 'In the morning we rose to perambulate a city, which only history shows to have once flourished, and surveyed the ruins of ancient magnificence, of which even the ruins cannot long be visible, unless some care be taken to preserve them; and where is the pleasure of preserving such mournful memorials? They have been till very lately so much neglected, that every man carried away the stones who fancied that he wanted them' (Johnson: 36).

Johnson went on to note that the cathedral 'was demolished, as is well known, in the tumult and violence of Knox's reformation' and that Beaton was murdered 'by the ruffians of reformation in the manner of which Knox has given what he himself calls a merry narrative'. He went on to deplore the 'epidemical enthusiasm, compounded of sullen scrupulousness and warlike ferocity' which had accompanied the change of religion from Catholic to Protestant in Scotland and noted sadly that 'the city of St Andrews, when it had lost its archiepiscopal pre-eminence, gradually decayed: one of its streets is now lost; and in those that remain, there is the silence and solitude of inactive indigence and gloomy depopulation'. He also deplored the fact that because the 'atrocious ravages' of the Reformation period had happened so long ago, they had largely been forgotten and consigned to ancient history: 'We read with as little emotion the violence of Knox and his followers, as the eruptions of Alaric and the Goths' (Johnson 1984: 36–9).

Like Dr Johnson, pilgrims coming to St Andrews today encounter many physical reminders of this distinctly violent and unedifying era

in its history. The massive cathedral, once the biggest and grandest in Scotland, stands roofless and ruined, as does the former bishops' palace known as the castle. Only a small part of the old Dominican house of Blackfriars remains, and nothing at all of the Franciscan friary. Perhaps as well as making it a city of ruins, the Reformation has left its mark on St Andrews by making it a place of empty niches. Again and again, I am struck going through its streets or into its buildings, particularly churches, of the number of niches and recesses which once housed statues but which are now bare and empty. You can see them on the substantial stretch of the old city walls enclosing the cathedral precincts, on the external buttresses of St Salvator's Chapel in North Street and above the archway that leads out of St Mary's College on to South Street. There are several very noticeable ones inside St Leonard's Chapel. In St Salvator's Chapel Bishop Kennedy's tomb has been stripped of all its decoration and ornamentation. There is nothing left of the thirty or more side altars dressed with cloth of gold and surmounted by gold crucifixes that once filled the interior of Holy Trinity Church. There is a bareness to many of the surviving ecclesiastical buildings that speaks both of the positive virtues of Protestant simplicity and of the negative consequences of excessive iconoclasm and determination to rid worship of idolatry.

There are other more recent physical reminders of St Andrews' role as the Reformation city. The site of George Wishart's death is marked by a blue plaque next to the ruined castle. In the middle of the cobbled pavement outside the University Chapel in North Street the initials PH, picked out in stones, mark the spot where Patrick Hamilton was slowly burned to death. Today's students carefully steer round the initials as stepping over them is regarded as bringing bad luck and specifically as risking failure in exams. On the Scores, the Martyrs' Monument, erected in 1843, the year of the Disruption which gave birth to the Free Church of Scotland, commemorates 'the martyrs Patrick Hamilton, Henry Forrest, George Wishart and Walter Mile [*sic*] who in support of the Protestant faith suffered death by fire at St Andrews'. Visitors passing this squat, stark obelisk, which is surely

Opposite
Empty niches
Above: St Mary's College gateway
Below: St Salvator's

one of the most striking architectural expressions of defiant Protestant identity anywhere in Britain, may well be impressed at its pristine appearance. It was expensively refurbished in 2013 thanks to a campaign spearheaded by preservation and heritage bodies under the umbrella of the St Andrews Partnership. It is perhaps worth noting that the Protestant churches of the town were somewhat embarrassed about this project. When I was approached by the St Andrews Partnership about the restoration project, I said I could and would only support it if there was an interpretation board acknowledging that Roman Catholics as well as Protestants were put to death for their faith in sixteenth-century Scotland and when I was asked to mastermind and devise a re-dedication ceremony for the newly refurbished memorial, I insisted that the local Roman Catholic priest take part alongside the Church of Scotland minister of the Town Kirk. Another architectural monument to St Andrews' role in the Reformation, Martyrs Kirk in North Street, which also dates from 1843 and was built as a Free Church to commemorate the martyrs, is now a university research library.

Visitors have sometimes said to me that they feel the streets of our small and beautiful city are still haunted by the legacy of this bloody and violent period when Christians killed each other in the name of their faith. For several years I have organised a walk of witness and prayer through the streets of St Andrews every Good Friday afternoon. We pause to reflect and pray at several of the sites associated with our troubled religious history. Initially, this walk involved just the congregations of the Church of Scotland parish churches but when I took it over I decided to invite the local Roman Catholic priest to join us. Standing in front of the castle, scene of so much hatred and violence, he publicly apologised for the atrocities committed by the Roman Catholic Church against Protestants in the past and spoke from the heart about the importance of people being able to follow their own consciences. I replied acknowledging that Protestants too did terrible things in this period and asking for forgiveness. I believe it touched all of us who were present, and it was one of the most moving personal experiences I have had in more than thirty years of living in St Andrews.

Opposite
Martyrs'
Monument

It is spontaneous ecumenical and eirenic gestures like these which begin to heal our wounds and bring us together as one in Christ. Our annual Good Friday pilgrimage through the town now involves leaders and members of virtually every local denomination. Perhaps our patron saint should be Thomas Methven, a priest attached to the Church of St Mary on the Rock, the ruins of which still provide an evocative reminder of St Andrews' Christian origins above the harbour and which is now the venue for an ecumenical dawn service every Easter Sunday morning. He refused to join the new Reformed Church when it was established in 1560 and found himself arraigned before the Kirk Session. 'I am neither a Papist nor a Protestant … but a Christian,' he told them. Amen to that – although I have to report that he ended up in Edinburgh as a lawyer, not the first nor the last man to be defeated by ecclesiastical in-fighting and denominational squabbling.

## II

# Under the archways and through the gates of the haunted town

St Andrews by the Northern sea,
A haunted town it is to me!
A little city, worn and grey,
The grey North Ocean girds it round,
And o'er the rocks, and up the bay,
The long sea-rollers surge and sound.
And still the thin and biting spray
Drives down the melancholy street,
And still endure, and still decay,
Towers that the salt winds vainly beat.
Ghost-like and shadowy they stand
Dim mirrored in the wet sea-sand.

So wrote the nineteenth-century poet and novelist Andrew Lang. He is not the only person to have found St Andrews to be a haunted place, perhaps even more than Oxford, whispering the last enchantments of the Middle Ages with its ruins and ghostly presences. The students at its world-famous university affectionately call it 'the Bubble'. It is also a tourist trap, luring ever more golfers to its famous courses, and a favourite place for the retired, second-home owners and buy-to-rent landlords who between them keep property prices high and have sadly pretty well forced many young local people and families to live out of town. Those coming as pilgrims at the end of traversing the Fife

Pilgrim Way will perhaps be most drawn to and interested in its rich heritage of spiritual sites and churches, and it is on these that this chapter will focus.

Exploring St Andrews, and especially its ecclesiastical and university buildings, involves constantly walking under arches or through gates. No other town that I know has as many of these striking and inviting architectural features. It is still possible to enter via the gates through which medieval pilgrims passed. Indeed, those walking the Fife Pilgrim Way will come through the West Port into South Street, taking the route that brought most medieval pilgrims to the cathedral. Those arriving by sea walked from the harbour up the road known as the Pends to enter the walled city through the magnificent double gateway erected around 1340 which still stands next to the cathedral ruins. Pend is an old Scottish word for an arch over an entry, so strictly speaking it is the gateway rather than the road leading to it that should bear this name. Most of the ancient university buildings and chapels and several of the town's many churches are similarly accessed by passing under arches and through gates.

Opposite
Above:
The West Port
Below:
Double gateway
at the Pends

Archways and gateways are liminal places which mark boundaries and lead us into new and unexpected territory and this is why they are particularly good to pass under or through as pilgrims. They take us from one world to another, giving us glimpses into new as yet untravelled ways and worlds and they frame our vistas.

Modern pilgrims should, like their medieval predecessors, go through the arches and the gateways of St Andrews thoughtfully, purposefully and reflectively, remembering that gates have often been the way into holy space and holy ground. So it was for the prophet Ezekiel, who was brought by God to the gate of the Temple, the holiest place in Jewish religion. As he stood there, Ezekiel had a vision in which the glory of the Lord entered the temple by the gate facing east, and the Spirit lifted him up and brought him into the inner court (Ezekiel 43: 1). So it was, too, for the author of Psalm 122, who rejoiced that 'our feet have been standing within your gates, Oh Jerusalem'. As we have already noted, St Andrews was compared to Jerusalem at the

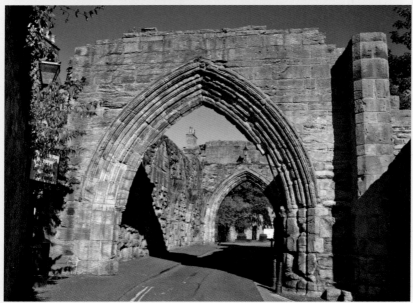

height of the pilgrimage boom in the Middle Ages. Medieval pilgrims passing through either the West Port or the Pends gateway from the harbour felt a stirring of spiritual anticipation as they entered the walled city. Something of that sense can still be captured today. The surviving remains of the wall that once surrounded medieval St Andrews are now almost entirely to be found in the vicinity of the harbour, with substantial stretches running along the northern edge of the cathedral precincts and enclosing what is now St Leonard's School along the side of the Shore and Abbey Walk. There are three fine gateways within this latter stretch of wall which are now largely closed, providing tantalising glimpses into hidden and secret places and serving as a reminder that not all avenues are open to us, and there are limits to our wandering.

Those entering the cathedral precincts today will probably either pass under the archway through the city wall that leads to the northern side of the sanctuary, near the base of the high altar, or through the modern gateway that leads to the great west entrance, itself a magnificent open stone doorway with its five receding orders of arches through which the equally mighty and imposing east gable is framed. There is a third way into the precincts through the archway halfway up the Pends which leads to the burial ground to the east of the cathedral. Once in the cathedral ruins, there are more arches to go under – to access what remains of the cloisters, St Rule's Church and tower and the priory buildings which include the refectory, chapter house, warming house and the vaulted refectory undercroft which now houses the cathedral museum and visitor centre.

Another of the buildings which was specifically built to cater for medieval pilgrims to St Andrews, St Leonard's Chapel, can be reached either through passing under the substantial archway halfway up the Pends from the harbour on the left-hand side, a few yards beyond the gateway on the other side leading to the cathedral burial ground, or through the open gateway off South Street leading to St Leonard's School. This chapel was part of the pilgrim hospice established by the Culdees and made over to the Augustinian monks running the cathedral

Opposite
St Leonard's
Chapel

in 1144. Its dedication is significant – Leonard, a Frankish noble who converted to Christianity in the late fifth century and declined a bishopric in favour of becoming a monk, and later a solitary hermit, was seen as the patron saint of travellers sheltering in inns and hospices, as well as of prisoners and midwives. The chapel also served as a second parish church for St Andrews (the first being Holy Trinity). It is first mentioned as 'the Kirk of St Leonard' in a document of 1413 but may well have had this role from the late twelfth century. Following its take-over by the university in the early sixteenth century, it became the chapel of the newly formed College of St Leonard as well as continuing as a parish church. Both of these roles continued beyond the Reformation.

In the mid eighteenth century St Leonard's College became a victim of the university's decline and its residential buildings passed into private hands. In the early 1880s they were taken over by the newly founded St Leonard's School, originally a girls' boarding school and now a co-educational boarding and day school, which still occupies them. The chapel was abandoned, with the kirk congregation transferring for worship to St Salvator's Chapel. Samuel Johnson was disturbed to find that the roofless chapel had been converted into 'a kind of green-house, by planting its area with shrubs. This new method of gardening is unsuccessful; the plants do not prosper'. Around 1853 Sir David Brewster, Principal of the university and a distinguished scientist as well as a Church of Scotland minister (although he only preached from a church pulpit once in his life), who lived very close to the ruined chapel, undertook substantial rebuilding work on the walls and turned the former sacristy into a wine-cellar. The chapel remained roofless and Andrew Lang, who lodged as a student nearby in the early 1860s, recalled:

St Leonard's Chapel, long ago
We loitered idly where the tall
Fresh budded mountain ashes blow
Within thy desecrated wall.

It was not until the early twentieth century that St Leonard's Chapel was rescued from its ruined state and restored for worship. In 1910 a new roof and windows were installed and in 1948 a scheme to renovate the interior was initiated by Sir David Russell, who ran and greatly expanded the family paper mill near Glenrothes (this became Tullis Russell and closed in 2015, see p. 153). The restored building was rededicated on St Leonard's Day 1952 in the first service to be held there for nearly 200 years. Although completely surrounded by the buildings of St Leonard's school, the chapel remains in the ownership of the university and is used for occasional services, notably for a candle-lit celebration of the ancient monastic office of compline which is held every Thursday evening during term time at 10 p.m., and to which all are welcome. Otherwise, sadly, it is generally locked.

St Leonard's Chapel serves as one of St Andrews University's two places of worship. The other, which is much bigger, more regularly used (including for the main university Sunday service at 11 a.m. during term time) and generally open to visitors during the hours of daylight, is St Salvator's Chapel in North Street. It is most easily accessed through the great archway under the adjoining tower (the tallest building in St Andrews) in front of which the initials PH mark the spot where Patrick Hamilton was burned to death. This archway also leads into the imposing main university quadrangle, which can also be entered through a gate halfway up the narrow lane known as Butts Wynd, under the arch that leads from the lawns below or via a much smaller gated archway from North Street at the eastern end of the chapel.

The Church of St Salvator, which was consecrated in 1460, served, like St Leonard's, both as a university chapel and as a parish kirk. It, too, had a long period of abandonment following the Reformation, in its case for 200 years from 1560, when it was rarely if ever used for religious services, with both university and town worshippers transferring to Holy Trinity Church. Both town and gown returned in 1761 to St Salvator's. In 1904 the St Leonard's Kirk congregation moved out to a new church built in the western residential area of the town and St

Salvator's became the official university chapel although it continues to attract as many townspeople as students and academics to its services.

Both inside and outside, the building retains much of its original fifteenth-century stonework. The interior has undergone successive alterations, not least in the aftermath of the Reformation, when the massive tomb of Bishop James Kennedy was stripped of much of its ornamentation. During the Middle Ages, the public nave at the west end was separated from the collegiate choir at the east by a screen similar to that now found in the reconstructed St Leonard's Chapel. This was removed after the Reformation, and subsequent nineteenth- and twentieth-century renovations have created an Oxbridge-style collegiate chapel with fixed tiered pews facing each other. A substantial west gallery built over the ante-chapel houses the chapel choir and the massive 3,000-pipe Hradetzky organ installed in 1974. The pulpit at the east end was moved from Holy Trinity Church and is sometimes said to be the one from which John Knox preached in the 1540s and 1550s, although experts are generally of the view that it is of a slightly later date. The marble communion table is faced with a mosaic of the Last Supper designed by Douglas Strachan, who was also responsible for the mosaics above it showing scenes in the life of Christ. Most of the stained-glass windows date from the early twentieth century.

Opposite
St Salvator's
Chapel
Above: Interior
Below: Bishop
Kennedy's tomb

The castle, which housed the bishops and archbishops of St Andrews for so long and played such a key role in the Scottish Reformation, is also worth visiting by those who have made their way to St Andrews along the Fife Pilgrim Way. It stands on a splendid clifftop site a few hundred yards west of the harbour. Most of the present structure dates from the sixteenth century but incorporates some stonework from the original castle built around 1200 by Bishop Roger as a residence for himself and his successors – previous bishops had resided in the cathedral priory. Captured and re-captured by Scots and English forces during the Wars of Independence, it lay neglected and in ruins for around fifty years before being rebuilt by Bishop Walter Traill at the end of the fourteenth century. The episcopal palace was probably at its most opulent and splendid during the archbishopric of James Beaton (1523–39), who is said to have provided livery for 120 horses in its precincts. Its key role in the bloody history of the Reformation at St Andrews has already been described (p. 227–9). Following its destruction by French cannon fire, it was rebuilt by Archbishop John Hamilton (1547–71), who added the handsome frontal range that can be seen from the street today. In 1587 an Act of the Scottish Parliament transferred the castle, along with other Church property, to the Crown. Although it briefly reverted to the Church in the seventeenth century, it fell into disuse, and in 1654 the town council ordered stones from the walls to be used for the repair of the harbour.

The castle is yet another building entered through a handsome archway – in its case accessed via a bridge over the moat (for long it was a drawbridge, as in all proper castles) – although visitors today have first to go via a modern entrance hall which houses an interesting historical exhibition. The castle is famous for its gloomy and forbidding bottle dungeon, a pit hollowed out of solid rock where, in John Knox's words, 'many of God's children were imprisoned', including Patrick Hamilton and George Wishart. Visitors can also inspect the mine and counter-mine tunnelled through the rock during the siege of 1546–7.

Another prominent gated archway in St Andrews leads from South Street to St Mary's College, the university's School of Divinity. Carved into the metalwork above its gate is text that forms the beginning of the prologue to St John's Gospel: *In Principio Erat Verbum*, 'In the beginning was the Word'. This is a particularly apt text for those entering university precincts, for universities are all about words – reading them, writing them, teaching them, researching them, memorising and savouring them. Over-arching them all, as over this gateway, is the Word with a capital W – the Logos, the Word made flesh, the great cosmic principle of order, harmony, reconciliation, forming order from chaos, embodied for Christians in the person of Jesus Christ. In the beginning was the Word, and Christians believe too that in the end is the Word, gathering all things up, the Alpha and the Omega. It is appropriate that this gate should have led students and professors into their studies of Divinity over an unbroken period

Opposite
Above:
The Castle
Below: St
Mary's College

of nearly five centuries since its foundation by papal bull in 1538 as 'a college of clerics, scholars and presbyters with a church or chapel under the invocation of the Blessed Virgin Mary, for the teaching of grammar, logic, natural philosophy, theology and canon and civil law', principally to provide well-educated priests to work in the archdiocese of St Andrews.

This particular gateway leads into one of the most beautiful and evocative quadrangles in St Andrews. Actually it is no longer a quadrangle – it used to be but all that remains on the far side is another rather fine gateway dating from the early fifteenth century and now surrounded by railings. This belonged to St John's College, the earliest part of the university, or the 'Pedagogy' as it seems to have been known. Near to it stands an imposing statue of the university's founder, Bishop Henry Wardlaw, in full episcopal vestments, proudly displaying the papal bull of foundation in his right hand and carrying his crozier in his left hand. A plaque below reads 'Henry Wardlaw, Bishop of St Andrews, 1403–1440. *Fundator Loci*'. Commissioned by the Strathmartine Trust under the tireless and enthusiastic prompting of Dr Barbara Crawford, the statue was sculpted by David Annand and unveiled on 29 June 2013 by Menzies Campbell, the Chancellor the university, as part of the programme of events to commemorate the sixth centenary of the university's foundation.

Opposite
Above: Bishop
Wardlaw statue
Below: St
Mary's

There is much else to see in St Mary's Quadrangle. It is dominated by the huge Holm oak known to have been planted in 1728. On the other side, in front of the entrance to the circular bell tower which houses two Divinity lecture rooms, are the remains of a thorn tree known as Queen Mary's thorn and said to have been planted by Mary, Queen of Scots. Temporarily blown down in a storm in 1893 and further damaged in 1974, it is now propped up by stays but remains still growing. There is an alternative hypothesis that the name of the tree refers to the Virgin Mary, to whom the college was dedicated. The empty niche above the gateway that leads back to South Street contained her image until it was removed at the Reformation. Immediately to the right of this gateway as you leave St Mary's is the King

James Library, the original university library, which was founded and endowed by James VI in 1612. On the other side, in the north-west corner of the quadrangle, is the elegant house which served as the residence of the college's principals from 1707 to 1978.

St Mary's College is in many ways the spiritual heart of the University. Divinity has been taught and studied here continuously since its foundation as 'the New College', as it became known to distinguish it from the earlier colleges of St Leonard's and St Salvator's, by Archbishop James Beaton in 1538. In its early days the college was very much under the direct control of the archbishops, first Beaton, then his nephew Cardinal David Beaton and his successor, Archbishop John Hamilton, who was largely responsible for laying out the present set of buildings in 1553 and whose coat of arms can be seen over the doorway that leads into the circular tower. Although it did not achieve its founders' aim of promoting a new reformed Catholicism robust enough to counter the Lutheranism taking root, especially in St Leonard's College, and preventing the wholesale Reformation that swept St Andrews and the whole of Scotland in the mid 1550s, the new college did establish certain principles – not least the teaching of biblical languages – that have remained important to this day. St Mary's remains a leading centre for biblical scholarship, with students taking classes in Hebrew and Greek and some even tackling Aramaic, the language spoken by Jesus himself.

St Mary's' first Protestant principal of note, Andrew Melville, who served in the role from 1580–1607, established the college as exclusively a school of Divinity and so it has remained ever since. Indeed it is now the only university department in Britain which is dedicated solely to the study of Christian theology and does not extend its scope to other religions. In other respects, St Mary's has changed considerably. For nearly four centuries following the Reformation it remained essentially what it had been at its foundation, a seminary for teaching clergy. Until sixty years or so ago its professors were almost exclusively ordained ministers of the Church of Scotland and its students were ordinands training for the same ministry. Now Church of Scotland ministerial candidates make up just a tiny proportion of the student body, many of whom combine theological or biblical studies with other disciplines and go on to a wide variety of careers.

On leaving St Mary's College to cross over South Street and begin our exploration of St Andrews' many churches with the parish church of the Holy Trinity, it is worth pausing under the richly decorated heraldic shield below a window on the grey outside wall. It bears the royal arms of Scotland, and specifically those of James V, having been painted in 1563, and so reinforces the close links between Church and State in Scotland. One of the explicit purposes for which St Mary's was founded was to offer perpetual prayers and masses for James IV and other members of the Scottish royal family. Relations between Church and Crown have not always been very cordial, as we have already seen. Andrew Melville is famous for telling James VI that he was God's silly vassal and reminding him that when it came to the Church, there was but one king, Christ Jesus, of whom he was merely a subject. Nonetheless, from Margaret onwards, Scotland's kings and queens have often been important spiritual leaders, promoting pilgrimage and helping to build Scotland's strong Christian character.

Holy Trinity Church, which lies diagonally across South Street from St Mary's College at the very centre of St Andrews, is entered under a modern wrought-iron archway surmounted by a lamp erected in memory of Maurice Wilson, a much-loved church officer in commemoration of his quiet and loyal service to Holy Trinity, the Boys' Brigade and the Order of St John. The church's origins go back at least as far as the mid twelfth century, when it was established as the parish kirk for those living within the burgh of St Andrews. It was originally sited in the shadow of the cathedral, close to its east end. Holy Trinity moved to its present site in the middle of the town in 1412. For the next 150 years until the Reformation it functioned as a major medieval Catholic church and contained more than thirty side chapels with altars, each served by a chaplain endowed by a local family or trade guild.

The Reformation, in which John Knox's sermons at Holy Trinity played so major a part, brought significant internal alterations, with the altars and chapels being removed and replaced by a single communion table and pews and side galleries facing a dominant pulpit. It remained the main parish church of the town, alternating between Episcopalianism and Presbyterianism throughout the seventeenth century and effectively being treated as a mini-cathedral by Archbishop Sharp. With Presbyterianism finally and firmly established as Scotland's national religion in 1689, the building was further altered to fit its word-centred worship. In the late 1780s further huge galleries were built across both the east and west ends and a larger three-decker pulpit installed. In the later nineteenth century Holy Trinity became a centre of High Church Presbyterian liturgical practices under the ministry of A.K.H. Boyd, who introduced controversial innovations such as hymn-singing. His successor, Patrick Playfair, commissioned the well-known Scoto-Catholic architect Peter Macgregor Chalmers to restore the church to something of its medieval grandeur and splendour. In what amounted to an almost wholesale rebuilding in 1907–9, the galleries were swept away, and the whole church opened up with large windows being installed. The huge pulpit was replaced by one made out of onyx and alabaster on a base of Iona marble erected as a memorial to Boyd, who was also commemorated by an elaborate font made out of Caen stone paid for by his children and erected near the west door to the church.

Opposite Great east window, Holy Trinity Church

All that remains of the fifteenth-century building today is the tower, part of the west wall and some of the pillars which support the great arches along the nave. Visitors and worshippers today generally enter the church through the John Knox porch which was built as part of the early twentieth-century renovations to commemorate the great Scots reformer. Like much of the church exterior, it has an abundance of carvings, including depictions of the Lamb of God surrounded by the four evangelists in winged form on the bosses in its roof. On the inside east wall of the porch are Knox's words: 'in this towne and churche began God first to call me to the dignitie of a precheour'. The great west door (in fact two doors surmounted by a

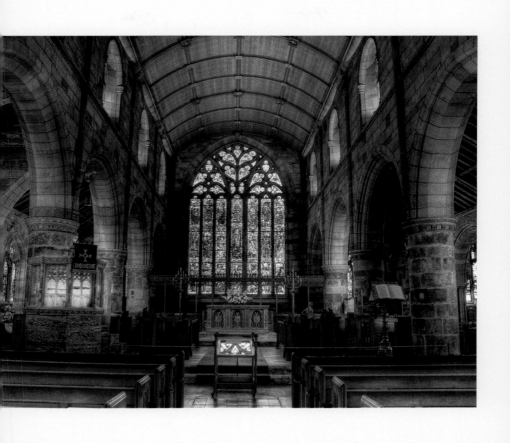

large arch), which is used for funerals and weddings, is said to be a memorial to two young people who were engaged to be married but both died before their wedding. On the outside central pillar between the two doorways is a carving of a pelican feeding its young with its own blood, a symbol of sacrifice, and on each side of the arch there is a small cherub, the one on the left holding the cross of salvation symbolising faith, the one on the right an anchor symbolising hope. Violets climb up the central pillar, symbolising innocence and purity, and the large arch surmounting the two doorways is decorated with the motif of a vine entwined with thorns.

Inside the church perhaps the most striking features are the superb stained-glass windows dating from the early twentieth century; these were designed and made by pioneers of the Arts and Crafts movement, notably the Aberdeen-born artist, Douglas Strachan. Particularly impressive are the great east window, based on the *Te Deum Laudamus*, the main window in the north transept, based on the *Benedicite Omnia Opera* and the great west window, celebrating the work and witness of women and the five cardinal female virtues of fidelity, faith, charity, hope and patience. St Margaret appears in a small 1968 window by Sax Shaw in the south transept, which is also known as the Sharp aisle because of its massive memorial to the murdered archbishop (see pp. 186–7). Windows high up in the clerestory above the nave depict the badges of the twelve Scottish regiments and of other branches of the British Armed Forces. They were gifted by those who had lost family members in the First World War.

There is much else to see and enjoy in the church, which resembles a mini-cathedral in its layout and size. A remnant of the medieval church survives in the form of two carved choir stalls dating from around 1500, and the harsh days of Presbyterian discipline are recalled by the branks, also known as the scold's bridle, an instrument of punishment for a scolding woman, consisting of an iron framework for the head and a sharp metal gag for restraining the tongue, and the stools of repentance, on which those found guilty of some sin or misdemeanour would be required to sit in full view of the congregation.

The tower of Holy Trinity was for many years used as the town's gaol and its bell sounded out a nightly curfew at 8 p.m. to remind inhabitants that they should be in their homes by then. It now houses one of Scotland's very few carillons, a set of twenty-seven bells which remain stationary in their frame and are struck by hammers operated by a system of wires and levers from a keyboard. The carillonneur strikes the keys, which resemble the shafts of golf clubs, with the outside of the hands and the heavier bells are activated by the feet via a pedal board.

At the time of writing there is some uncertainty as to the long-term future of this beautiful and historically important church. Falling numbers of members and worshippers and the ever-rising costs of insurance, heating, lighting and maintenance have made it potentially financially unviable and the congregation is not at present being allowed to call a full-time minister. Efforts are currently under way to assess the viability of creating a Town Kirk Trust which might conceivably take over ownership of the building from the Church of Scotland, and to explore possible revenue-raising activities that might take place within it while still keeping it as a place of Christian worship.

It may be that the coming of more pilgrims in St Andrews with the opening of the Fife Pilgrim Way will create opportunities for this and other churches in the town to become places of welcome and hospitality. Given its location and history, Holy Trinity would certainly make a splendid venue for a pilgrim welcome centre, providing inter-pretation of the religious history of St Andrews and facilitating explo-ration of the wider spiritual ramifications of pilgrimage. It must also surely remain a centre of Christian worship.

Already another of St Andrews' parish churches has found alter-native use as a place of educational research. Martyrs Kirk, which was built as a Free Church in 1843 by the group which split away from the established Church over patronage and then came back into the Church of Scotland with the reunion of 1929, was closed in 2008 and subse-quently bought by the University of St Andrews, which has turned it into a reading room for postgraduates. The former Salvation Army citadel next door in North Street suffered a rather worse fate, being turned in 2016 into a beer kitchen. Poor old General Booth, the Salvation Army's founder who was committed to teetotalism, must have turned in his grave at this change of use. However, the man who famously asked why the Devil should have all the good tunes may yet have the last laugh. The Beer Kitchen survived for just eighteen months before it closed, whereas the Salvation Army occupied the premises for twenty years. At the time of writing, the future of this building is not clear, although I doubt very much that it will revert to a religious use and purpose. The fate of these two adjoining former places of worship pays eloquent if melancholy testimony to the strange death of Protestantism in the town which cradled the Scottish Reformation.

St Andrews' other two Church of Scotland parish churches are in better health. Hope Park, originally built in 1865 as a United Presbyterian church, stands opposite the bus station welcoming pilgrims who choose to come by that route. Linked with the former Martyrs Kirk, its interior layout is a classic expression of Reformed worship, with galleries ranged on three sides around the focal point, a massive pulpit standing against the east wall behind a small communion table. St Leonard's Church, built in 1904 at the corner of Hepburn Gardens and Donaldson Gardens in the residential west end of the town to accommodate the congregation that had for so long worshipped in the old St Leonard's Kirk and then in St Salvator's, was designed, like the new Holy Trinity, by Peter Macgregor Chalmers and shows Romanesque influence, especially in the circular apses housing the communion table and the font. Unusually, the choir stalls are situated in a side aisle at the back of the church, which has some good early twentieth-century stained-glass windows, one of which inspired me to write a lengthy theological tome about the power of sacrifice. By coming off the Lade Braes opposite the entrance to Cockshaugh Park, and crossing over Hepburn Gardens, modern pilgrims can see this church and also visit the museum in Kinburn Park, with its display of pilgrim badges, before heading for the West Port.

*Opposite St Leonard's Church*

The Roman Catholic Church dedicated to St James, the patron saint of pilgrims, has a wonderful situation on the Scores, perched on the cliffs overlooking the sea and the West Sands. Designed by Reginald Fairlie in Arts and Crafts style in 1910 to replace an earlier corrugated iron building, it has some good modern windows, prominently depicting St Andrew, St Margaret and, somewhat bizarrely, the Orcadian St Magnus. Columba and Mungo are relegated to a small window in a side chapel, but it is at least good to see one of the two saints whom we set out with from Culross acknowledged at the end of the pilgrimage. There are a couple of Episcopalian churches in the town. St Andrews in Queen's Terrace, which was built in 1869, is something of a barn. More interesting architecturally is All Saints Church, sited near the castle in North Castle Street. Its chancel and bell tower date from 1907 and the church was greatly extended in the early 1920s thanks to the generosity of Annie Younger, who intended it especially to minister to the many fisher folk in the east end of the town and also endowed a complex of buildings which included a gymnasium, halls for amateur theatricals and for use by guides, women's and men's club rooms, a library and a billiard room. The whole complex is entered through a small and beautiful courtyard via a fine wrought-iron gate decorated with colourful images of vine leaves and grapes and installed in 1957 to replace an earlier gate and railings which were removed during the Second World War to provide metal for guns and armaments. Describing the overall architectural style of the church and its associated buildings, John Gifford wrote 'the idiom is Scottish vernacular, the flavour gay Italian' (Gifford 1988: 378).

The interior of All Saints, which is usually open to visitors, exudes an atmosphere of holiness and piety and is a good place for quiet contemplation and holy rest. It is full of interesting artistic objects, including a carving of the Virgin and child by the distinguished twentieth-century Scottish sculptor Hew Lorimer, an elaborate font with a gilded wood cover housed in a baptistery with an impressive wrought-iron screen and an elaborate side chapel, the entrance to which is flanked by marble pillars surmounted by kneeling angels.

There are good stained-glass windows, including several by Douglas Strachan. Perhaps the most significant for pilgrims is the window on the north side designed by Karl Parsons and entitled 'For All the Saints', which portrays a galaxy of Irish, Scottish and Anglo-Saxon saints grouped around the Madonna and child, including Bridget, Kentigern, Andrew, Wilfrid, Columba, Ninian, Margaret and Patrick and the less well-kent figures of Mund, Kennocha, Maura and Medana.

The Baptists have a neat little church in South Street dating from 1842 but have for many years preferred to hold their Sunday morning worship in the Kilrymont buildings of the local secondary school, Madras College. St Andrews' newer denominations, the Free Church, Cornerstone and Vineyard Fellowship, which attract large numbers of students and younger people, do not have designated buildings but prefer to meet for worship in schools, halls and other premises around the town. It may well be that the future of Christian worship lies in forsaking old, expensive and draughty buildings in favour of this more provisional and pilgrim-like approach. The decision by these newer churches not to commit substantial resources to fabric and buildings brings a flexibility which is perhaps more in keeping with the idea of the church as a movement rather than an institution and with the way in which early Christians described themselves as people on and of the Way.

Perhaps Christian witness in St Andrews most reflects this ethos of a pilgrim church when people of the many different denominations in the town come together and worship outside. I have already mentioned the annual Good Friday pilgrimage, which has grown from being just a Church of Scotland enterprise into one that is fully ecumenical and involves virtually all of the town's churches. We walk, carrying a cross, starting from St Mary's College and then going to the ruined Blackfriars Chapel in South Street, the Market Square, the site of Patrick Hamilton's martyrdom in front of St Salvator's Chapel, Martyrs' Monument on the Scores, the castle and site of George Wishart's death on the cliffs, the town's war memorial in front of the cathedral, and ending up at the ruins of St Mary's on the Rock.

There, on what was almost certainly the site of the oldest Christian settlement in the area, the cross is laid down. On Easter Sunday morning there is an ecumenical dawn service on the same spot, where several hundred people gather round the cross, which has remained there, empty and alone, for thirty-six hours or more. For some years, we went on to hold an Easter Sunday Eucharist from the base of the former altar in the ruined cathedral nave. The establishment of the Fife Pilgrim Way should provide many more opportunities for similar open-air services and gatherings, both at points along the route and within St Andrews. I have led many groups on a prayer walk around the town, during which we pause at some of the many significant religious sites to think both about their history and their spiritual significance. It will be particularly good if pilgrims can make use of the cathedral and its precincts both for personal and spontaneous small-group devotions and for much bigger organised acts of worship, as Catholic pilgrim groups like New Dawn and the Confraternity of St Ninian already do.

St Andrews Cathedral is the natural end-point for those undertaking the Fife Pilgrim Way, although pilgrims arriving after it has closed for the day may wish to end their journey either opposite its west front on the cobbled area in front of Dean's Court or overlooking the harbour on the headland where the first Christian settlement in the area was probably located and the Church of St Mary's on the Rock subsequently erected. Even in its ruined state, the cathedral still dominates the eastern end of the town. The surviving parts, which are essentially the great east and west fronts, the south transept and south nave walls together with the bases of piers in the nave and choir, are enough to give a strong impression of just how imposing the building must have been when it was complete. It was only supplanted as the largest building in Scotland with the construction of Edinburgh's Waverley Station in 1868. There have periodically been calls for it to be restored to its former glory. Some idea of what the end result of such a project would look like can be gained from the virtual reconstruction of the cathedral in its heyday, made by historians and computer scientists

Digital reconstruction of St Andrews Cathedral

working for St Andrews University's Open Virtual Worlds.

In the late 1990s the Scottish artist and impresario Richard Demarco proposed rebuilding the cathedral as a national shrine to Scotland's patron saint. He commended it as a comparable project to the restoration of Iona Abbey and its associated monastic buildings by George MacLeod in the 1930s and the rebuilding of Coventry Cathedral after its destruction through bombing in the Second World War. Perhaps if the members of every Christian denomination and congregation in St Andrews and the surrounding area, of which there are more than twenty, agreed to forsake and close their own buildings and to worship together in a restored cathedral, there might be some justification for such a huge and costly project. But that is unlikely to happen, I fear. And maybe there is something positive and symbolic about keeping its nave and sanctuary open to the sky above, with the gulls swooping through the arches and the wind dancing in from the sea as a reminder of the totality and physicality of God's creation and the impermanence of all human institutions.

Christians in Britain are coming to the end of a thousand-year era, inaugurated by the Normans, of building great temples of stone designed to last for centuries. These buildings, of which St Andrews Cathedral in its medieval heyday was a towering example, continue to speak of the permanence of eternal things and preach their sermons in stone down the generations. However, many old churches are a millstone around the necks of their congregations, the cost of their upkeep and repair diverting funds and attention from the more vital tasks of mission and social action. Newer, growing Christian groups, like those in St Andrews, are dispensing with such purpose-built structures and meeting in more temporary shelters which can be adapted and discarded as circumstances change. In this way they are emulating the ancient Israelites, who felt closer to God when they carried a portable tabernacle on their wanderings through the desert than when they later pinned the Almighty down by building the massive stone temple in Jerusalem.

It is perhaps appropriate that the Fife Pilgrim Way ends quite literally in ruins. Just like the logo based on the pilgrim badge with its missing right side, they speak of the brokenness and pain of the human condition and of pilgrimage. The fact that St Andrews Cathedral is not pristine and complete but lacking a roof and furnishings and open to the elements reminds us of the incompleteness and impermanence of all human institutions, and indeed of our own lives. Here, as the Epistle to the Hebrews states, we have no abiding city and no permanent abode. Passing through the gateways and under the arches of the haunted town of St Andrews may well give us glimpses of eternity and lead us, like Ezekiel, to holy ground and places filled with the glory of the Lord. But we are only passing through them, as we have passed through so many other fascinating and evocative places and landscapes on the Fife Pilgrim Way. We reach the end point of our journey – in this case the ruined cathedral – only to set out again and return. As T.S. Eliot observed in *The Four Quartets*, the end is where we start from.

# Conclusion:
# The end ... and the beginning

You who have traversed the Fife Pilgrim Way, whether on foot or bicycle, by car, bus or train or simply through reading this book, have passed through many kinds of landscape and had many experiences. You have set out with the saints from the waters of the Forth and savoured something of monastic life with its rhythm of solitude and community and its balance of prayer, study, meditation and manual labour. You have travelled through former coal-mining communities, with their sense of solidarity and sacrifice and their legacy of depression and decline. You have breathed in the beauty of the gentle hills and broad farmland of north-east Fife and felt the unique atmosphere of the haunted town that has beckoned pilgrims for over a thousand years. You have passed through a wide variety of human habitations, from the picture-postcard villages of Culross and North Queensferry, through gritty and impoverished urban streets and douce rural hamlets to the tourist honey-pot of affluent St Andrews.

Opposite Bloodyfoots path, near Kinglassie

Pilgrimage is about much more than just travelling through different landscapes. One of the emphases in this book has been on walking alongside people, whether actually in terms of your companions and those whom you meet along the way, or through the imagination in terms of those in whose footsteps you have been following. Susan Brown, Moderator of the General Assembly of the Church of Scotland from 2018–19, took 'walking alongside people' as the theme of her moderatorial year; she has written that 'When you walk alongside people, you listen and exchange stories … It gives the chance to talk more deeply than when we are face to face … I want to encourage people to get out more because while it can be one of the hardest things to do when you are depressed, it is also very healing' (see *Life and Work*, December 2017, p. 39).

You have had many invisible companions along this particular pilgrim way – Serf, Mungo, Margaret, Willie Gallacher, James Sharp, John Knox, Patrick Hamilton, James Beaton and the many other characters mentioned in these pages who have played their part in the rich religious, social and political history of Fife. You have in your imaginations meditated with monks, marched with miners, been moved by the faith of martyrs, and maybe slightly repelled by the fanaticism of the Covenanters and their persecutors. Perhaps you have been challenged or even changed by something or someone that you have encountered on the journey. Maybe it was the story of self-sacrifice on the part of young George Paton in 1916, as recorded in the plaque on the path between North Queensferry and Inverkeithing as it runs alongside the Forth (see p. 62). Maybe it was the sculpture of the mother with her baby and small son awaiting news from the pithead, which commemorates the explosion in the Valleyfield pit in 1939 that killed thirty-five miners (see p. 116). Maybe it was George Wishart's words of forgiveness to those who were putting him to death (see p. 226). One of the differences between tourists and pilgrims is that the former tend simply to pass through places while the latter let places, and people, pass through, influence and affect them. I hope this has happened to you.

And now at the end of your pilgrimage, you pause and then turn round to return, back home or back to work with all its familiar routines and frustrations and preoccupations. Pilgrimage is about setting out, only to come back again. As in life, we depart only to return. Our lives involve a series of journeys out and back until we make our final pilgrimage into the unknown region that lies beyond death. Maybe even after death our pilgrimages and our journeys continue and we are still on the Way and just beginning to set out again. Travel well and remember, as Jerome said, *solvitur ambulando* (it can be solved by walking).

# Select bibliography

Anderson, A.O. (ed.), *Early sources of Scottish history, A.D. 500 to 1286*, Vols I & II (Edinburgh: Oliver and Boyd, 1922)

Anderson, Marjorie, *Kings and kingship in early Scotland* (Edinburgh: Scottish Academic Press, 1980)

Atherton, David, & Peyton, Michael, *Saint Margaret, patroness of Scotland* (http://saintsandrelics.co.uk/onewebmedia/ St.%20Margaret.pdf, March 2016)

Auchterderran Church Congregation, *Auchterderran Kirk 2016* (2016: Auchterderran)

Ballingall, William, *The kingdom of Fife in days gone by* (Edinburgh: Edmonston & Douglas, 1872)

Barr, Leslie, *Discovering our roots: a brief history of the Presbyterian churches in Kelty* (Kelty: Church Office, 2007)

Bartlett, Robert (ed.), *The miracles of Saint Aebbe of Coldingham and Saint Margaret of Scotland* (Oxford: Clarendon Press, 2003)

Brown, Michael & Stevenson, Katie (eds), *Medieval St Andrews: church, cult, city* (Woodbridge: Boydell Press, 2017)

Buckroyd, Julia, *The Life of James Sharp* (Edinburgh: John Donald, 1987)

Campbell, Ian, 'Planning for pilgrims: St Andrews as the second Rome', *Innes Review* (2013) 64:1, pp. 1–22

Cooney, Les & Maxwell, Alex, *No more bings in Benarty* (Benarty Mining Heritage Group, 1992)

Dawson, Jane, *John Knox* (New Haven: Yale University Press, 2015)

Dove, Giles, *Saints, Dedications and cults in medieval Fife* (University of St Andrews MPhil thesis, 1988)

Durland, Kellogg, 'Among the Fife miners', *Blackwood's Magazine*, Vol. 171, 1902

Durland, Kellogg, *Among the Fife miners* (London: Swan Sonnenschein, 1904)

Fawcett, Richard (ed.), *Royal Dunfermline* (Edinburgh: Society of Antiquaries of Scotland, 2005)

Gifford, John, *The buildings of Scotland: Fife* (London: Pevsner Architectural Guides, 1988)

Hall, Ursula, *St Andrew and Scotland* (St Andrews: University Library, 1994)

Hollis, Patricia, *Jennie Lee: a Life* (Oxford University Press, 1997)

Hutton, Guthrie, *Fife: The mining kingdom* (Catrine: Stenlake, 1999)

Johnson, Samuel, *A journey to the Western Isles of Scotland* (London: Penguin Books, 1984)

Knox, John, *The history of the Reformation in Scotland* (Edinburgh: Banner of Truth Trust, 1982)

Laing, David, *Historie of the Estate of Scotland, From July 1558 to April 1560* (Edinburgh: Woodrow Society, 1844)

Lamont-Brown, Raymond, *Discovering Fife* (Edinburgh: John Donald, 1988)

Lyon, C.J., *History of St Andrews* (Edinburgh: William Tait, 1843, 2 vols)

MacDougall, Ian (ed.), *Militant miners; recollections of John McArthur, Buckhaven; and letters, 1924–6, of David Proudfoot, Methil* (Edinburgh: Polygon Books, 1981)

Mackay, A.J.G., *A history of Fife and Kinross* (Edinburgh: William Blackwood, 1896)

MacQuarrie, Alan, *The saints of Scotland* (Edinburgh: John Donald, 1997)

MacQuarrie, Alan (ed.), *Legends of the Scottish saints: readings, hymns and prayers for the commemoration of Scottish saints in the Aberdeen Breviary* (Dublin: Four Courts Press, 2012)

Manson, Bruce, *MacDuff's Kirk? The construction and reconstruction of St Drostan's Church Markinch* (Markinch: Pittanhaigles Press, 2017)

Menzies, Lucy, *St Margaret, Queen of Scotland* (reprint Llanerch: Felinfach, 1992)

Millar, A.H., *Fife: pictorial and historical*, Vols I & II (Cupar: A. Westwood & Son, 1895)

Muirhead, Andrew, *Reformation, dissent and diversity: the story of Scotland's churches, 1560–1960* (London: Bloomsbury, 2015)

Nasaw, David, *Andrew Carnegie* (New York: Penguin Books, 2007)

*New Statistical Account of Scotland*, Vol. 9 (Edinburgh: William Blackwood, 1845)

Omand, Donald (ed.), *The Fife book* (Edinburgh: Birlinn, 2000)

Rhodes, Elizabeth, 'The Reformation in the Burgh of St Andrews: Property, Piety and Power' (unpublished PhD thesis, University of St Andrews, 2013)

Robertson, Mima, *Old Dunfermline* (Edinburgh: Paul Harris Publishing, 1979)

Simpkins, John Ewart (ed.), *County folklore, vol. VII: Fife* (London: Sidgwick & Jackson, 1914)

Skene, William, *Johannis de Fordun Chronica Gentis Scotorum*, Vol. 1 (Edinburgh: Edmonston & Douglas, 1871)

Stephen, William, *History of Inverkeithing and Rosyth* (Aberdeen: G. & W. Fraser, 1921)

Taylor, Simon & Márkus, Gilbert, *The place names of Fife*, Vols 1–5 (Donington: Shaun Tyas, 2006–12).

Turgot, *The Life of Margaret, Queen of Scotland*, ed. William Forbes-Leith (Edinburgh: David Douglas, 1896)

Turpie, Tom, *Kind neighbours : Scottish saints and society in the later Middle Ages* (Leiden: Brill, 2015)

Turpie, Tom, 'Fife Pilgrim Way project: report detailing historical references to pilgrimage and the cult of saints in medieval Fife' (unpublished paper prepared for the FPW steering group, 1 September 2016)

Wall, Joseph Frazier, *Andrew Carnegie* (New York: Oxford University Press, 1970)

Watt, Donald (ed.), *Scotichronicon in Latin and English*, Vols I–IX (Aberdeen: Aberdeen University Press, 1987–99)

Westwood, Jennifer & Kingshill, Sophia, *The lore of Scotland: a guide to Scottish legends* (London: Random House, 2009)

Yeoman, Peter, *Pilgrimage in medieval Scotland* (London: Batsford/Historic Scotland, 1999)

# Useful Information

Whilst this is a companion rather than a guidebook, the following pages provide information which those actively undertaking all or part of the Fife Pilgrim Way may find useful. Every effort has been made to check these details, and they are believed to be correct at time of publication – no responsibility can be taken for subsequent changes.

**Maps covering the route**
A detailed map showing the entire route of the Fife Pilgrim Way and a pilgrim's passport are available from outlets along the route and also directly from Fife Coast and Countryside Trust, The Harbourmaster's House, Hot Pot Wynd, Dysart, Kirkcaldy KY1 2TQ, phone: 01592 656080, website: *www.fifecoastandcountrysidetrust.co.uk*

The route is covered by the following Ordnance Survey maps:

*First section* (Culross and North Queensferry to Dunfermline)
OS Landranger 65
Falkirk & Linlithgow

*Second section* (Dunfermline to Leslie)
OS Landranger 58
Perth & Alloa

*Third section* (Leslie to St Andrews)
OS Landranger 59
St Andrews, Kirkcaldy & Glenrothes

**Pilgrim websites**
Fife Pilgrim Way website: *www.fifecoastandcountrysidetrust.co.uk/Fife-Pilgrim-Way*
Fife Pilgrim Way Facebook page: *www.facebook.com/Fife-Pilgrim-Way*
Scottish Pilgrim Routes Forum website: *www.sprf.org.uk*

**Information centres, museums, libraries and heritage centres on or close to the route (and often providing toilets!)**

**Culross**
Culross Abbey
Kirk Street
Culross KY12 8JD
*www.culrossabbey.co.uk*
*www.historicenvironment.scot/visit-a-place/places/culross-abbey*

Culross Palace (National Trust for Scotland)
Blair Castle
Culross
KY12 8JH
01383 880359
*www.nts.org.uk/visit/places/culross*

## Valleyfield
Valleyfield Library
Chapel St
Valleyfield
Dunfermline KY12 8JH
01383 880683
*www.onfife.com/venues/valleyfield-library*

## Inverkeithing
Inverkeithing Civic Centre
10 Queen Street
Inverkeithing
KY11 1PA
01383 602471
*www.onfife.com/venues/inverkeithing-library-and-heritage-centre*

## Dunfermline
Dunfermline Abbey and Palace (Historic Environment Scotland)
St Margaret's Street
Dunfermline KY12 7PE
01383 739026
*www.historicenvironment.scot/visit-a-place/places/dunfermline-abbey-and-palace*

Dunfermline Abbey (Church of Scotland)
Dunfermline, KY12 7PE
01383 724586
*www.dunfermlineabbey.com/wwp*
*www.historicenvironment.scot/visit-a-place/places/dunfermline-abbey-and-palace*

St Margaret's Cave
Glen Bridge Car Park
Chalmers St
Dunfermline KY12 8DF
01383 602386
*www.onfife.com/venues/st-margarets-cave*

Carnegie Birthplace Museum
Moodie St
Dunfermline KY12 7PL
01383 724302
*www.carnegiebirthplace.com*

Carnegie Library and Galleries
1–7 Abbot St
Dunfermline KY12 7NW
01383 602365
*www.onfife.com/venues/dunfermline-carnegie-library-galleries*
*www.facebook.com/ONatDCLG/*

**Kelty**
Kelty Library & Community Centre
90-92 Main St
Kelty KY4 0AE
01383 602367
*www.onfife.com/venues/kelty-library*

**Lochore Meadows**
Lochore Meadows Country Park
Crosshill
Lochgelly KY5 8BA
01592 583343
*www.lochoremeadows.org.uk*

## Leslie

Leslie Library
289 High Street
Leslie
KY6 3AX
01592 583601
*www.onfife.com/venues/leslie-library*

## Glenrothes

Rothes Hall Library
Kingdom Shopping Centre
Glenrothes
KY7 5NX
01592 583387
*www.onfife.com/venues/rothes-halls-library*

## Kennoway

Kennoway Library
1 Bishop's Ct
Kennoway
Leven KY8 5LA
01334 659372
*www.onfife.com/venues/kennoway-library*

## Ceres

Fife Folk Museum
High St
Ceres
Cupar KY15 5NF
01334 828180
*www.fifefolkmuseum.org*

**St Andrews**
St Andrews Cathedral (Historic Environment Scotland)
The Pends
St Andrews KY16 9QL
01334 472536
*www.historicenvironment.scot/visit-a-place/places/*
*st-andrews-cathedral*

St Andrews Castle (Historic Environment Scotland)
The Scores
St Andrews KY16 9AR
01334 477196
*www.historicenvironment.scot/visit-a-place/places/st-andrews-castle*

St Andrews Museum
Kinburn Park
Doubledykes Road
St Andrews KY16 9DP
01334 659380
*www.onfife.com/venues/st-andrews-museum*

Visit Scotland Tourist Information Centre
70 Market St
St Andrews
KY16 9NU
01334 472021
*www.visitscotland.com*

# Index of People and Places